ENDORSEMENTS

"Kevin Sweeney's *The Joy of Letting Go* is a vulnerable, wise, brave, accessible book; the rare transformational work that will actually change you if you open yourself up to it. The path toward life feels a whole lot like dying, but "letting go" is the only thing that liberate us--and the joy on the other side of surrender truly is as profound as the pain. Don't just read this book--give in to the truth that you will feel rumbling underneath it; let it take you where you need to go."

— **Jonathan Martin**, Author of *The Road Away from God* and *How to Survive a Shipwreck*, Chaplain at DePauw University

"With his rhythmic and relational writing style, Kevin Sweeney gently invites us to see the importance of letting go as a regular practice throughout our spiritual journey. He gracefully reminds us that much of life involves this practice and emphasizes its importance in order to receive what's before us within the present moment. I'm deeply grateful for the playful and profound wisdom Kevin offers us in this book."

— **Holly K. Oxhandler, PhD, LMSW**; associate dean for research and associate professor at Baylor University's Garland School of Social Work, and author of *The Soul of the Helper*

"The commodification of the spiritual life has created a kind of spirituality that taps into our desire for achievement, possession and notoriety. Sweeney offers a vision that is counter to that, offering instead a roadmap towards more peace and wholeness. You can trust him to be your guide in this terrain, because has been living it. He writes out of his deep well of study and experience in order to open us up to live with more freedom and joy. The Joy of Letting Go is a helpful invitation to honestly investigate what you are holding onto and what it is keeping you from."

— **Mike Goldsworthy**, author of *In God We Trust?* and co-creator of "The Post-Evangelical Collective"

"In *The Joy of Letting Go*, Sweeney shows us that letting go is the gateway to an abundant and meaningful life. As I read this book, I found myself being filled with hope and ideas that I couldn't wait to write down so I could consider them for days and weeks to come."

— **Nick Laparra**, environmentalist, speaker, investigative journalist, and host of "Let's Give a Damn" podcast

THE JOY OF LETTING GO

HOW **ONE THING** HAS THE POWER TO CHANGE **EVERYTHING**

KEVIN SWEENEY

All rights reserved. No part of this book may be used or reproduced, stored in a retrieval system, or transmitted in any form or by any means, electronic, mechanical, photocopying, recording, scanning, or otherwise, without written permission from the publisher except in the case of brief quotations embodied in critical articles and reviews. Permission for wider usage of this material can be obtained through Quoir by emailing permission@quoir.com.

Copyright © 2023 by Kevin Sweeney

First Edition

ISBN 978-1-957007-36-6

This volume is printed on acid free paper and meets ANSI Z39.48 standards. Printed in the United States of America

QUOIR

Published by Quoir
Chico, California
www.quoir.com

To Rafael,

May you know joy through this chapter of letting go.
I could never thank you enough.

CONTENTS

ACKNOWLEDGMENTS	vii
INTRODUCTION	ix
1. BEING PRESENT	1
2. BEGINNING AGAIN	15
3. COMPASSION	31
4. EXPERIENCING GOD AND RECEIVING LOVE	47
5. GROWING AND EVOLVING	63
6. PEACE	81
7. WORKING FOR JUSTICE	97
8. ACCEPTANCE	113
9. WELCOME AND INCLUSION	125
10. CREATIVITY/MAKING	143
11. INNER AUTHORITY	157
12. JOY	173
13. FORGIVENESS	187
14. OUTRO	203
BOOKS REFERENCED	206

ACKNOWLEDGMENTS

Christine for the support and courage to keep growing together.

Mikayla and True for everything you are.

Rod for your friendship and support.

Livvy for risking it all for me with the scanner.

Jade for your expertise and dedication (sorry for last minute message!)

Imagine Church for allowing us to let go into grace.

Matt and Keith for welcoming me to the future.

INTRODUCTION

To begin, I just want you to know that I know.

I know writing an entire book about letting go is not a great strategy for gaining popularity or building a platform.

I know that we want thoughts on being brave, new ways to think about God, and the permission to allow our lives to be unfinished and messy. And I know that if we're honest, we aren't that interested in reading about acceptance, dying, and letting go. And if we are really honest, we are even less interested in actually doing these things.

I know that letting go is the least inspirational topic and the last thing we want.

I know that.

But knowing this creates an ever present dilemma for me as a writer and for us as humans.

For me, it means I only want to write about the one thing people don't want anything to do with.

For us as people, it means we are uninterested or unwilling to do the one thing that has the power to give us everything.

Which is, of course, letting go.

When one of the great living mystics, Father Richard Rohr, writes, "All great spirituality is somehow about letting go," do we just skim by this and catalogue it as another great quotable by a prolific author?

Or, do we dare to allow this truth to utterly change our relationship with God, humanity, and reality itself? Can we feel the truth of this statement resonate in the center of our being so powerfully that we are almost forced to ask the natural question that follows:

How?

How is each life altering step of the great spiritual journey somehow about letting go?

Well, this book is the answer to that question.

Here is where I begin: virtually every time we are angry, feel stuck, and are struggling to move forward—of course after all of the rage, blame, name calling, threats, pity parties, and explosive outrage at God and life itself subsides—eventually, there is probably just something we need to let go of.

We fight, we resist, and we desperately try to believe it is a million other easier things than the one thing it almost always ends up being—we need to do some letting go.

Sucks.

I know.

We'd rather get angrier at injustice and rage against the machine harder.

We'd rather just show up at the next event and sing louder.

We'd rather read another book about letting go and try to figure it out in our minds.

We wish we could simply move faster, work harder, or become more determined. But after all of those impulses fire off in our body, and each of those desires race by our stream of consciousness, eventually, there's probably something painful we need to accept.

Which means there is something else we need to let go of.

Like I said. Sucks.

And yet, no matter how much it sucks or how painful it is, what we always discover on the other side of letting go is a new beginning.

Every time you let go, you begin again.

And every time you begin again, a part of you is born again.

***

When I started graduate school at twenty four years old, I was convinced that I was going to be in school for three years, finish both of my degrees, and then go straight into a PhD program. And with no surprise, that trajectory started to unfold for me. I connected with the one professor who I wanted to work with more than any other (shout out Doc Watkins), he asked me to write a chapter for his up and coming book, and as the years went on, he committed to be the advisor for my doctoral work.

Everything was going the way I wanted and my plans were coming together exactly as I anticipated.

Which means you know exactly what happened next.

KEVIN SWEENEY

Yep.

It all fell apart.

At the end of the summer before my last year of grad school, my wife and I were headed to surf at Newport Beach. We pulled into a 7-11 gas station, and as the gas was filling, I reached down to grab my Blackberry (you can guess what year this was based on the phone), and when I read my most recent e-mail, my mind, heart, and body immediately aligned with this sense of shock.

By the time I was done reading, it felt like I was standing in the debris of a burnt down city, wondering what I was supposed to do next.

My mentor and future PhD advisor was leaving the school.

He could not take on any new projects he had not started yet.

Which meant he could no longer be my advisor. Which also meant my plan for the next five years had vanished in an instant.

The bridge to my vocational future just collapsed, and with no warning at all, I was suddenly free falling into an abyss, and had no idea what I was going to do with my life or how I could help support my family in the future.

For the next two hours, I just sat on my board in the water, watching the waves roll by, with barely any desire to even paddle and catch any.

A couple days later as I was going to spend time in silence with the intention of being fully present to what was happening within me, I felt deeply compelled to bring one of my Thomas Merton books. I had this deep sense there was something in there for me.

After I sat down and did my breathing, I turned a few pages and got wonderfully drawn to this short statement.

"We must learn to realize that the love of God seeks us in every situation, and seeks our good. His inscrutable love seeks our awakening. True, since this awakening implies a kind of death to our exterior self, we will dread His coming in proportion as we are identified with this exterior self and attached to it."

We will "dread the incoming of Christ" to the degree we are attached to and identified with our exterior or false self—along with all of its desires, plans, and particularities.

It was everything I needed to see.

Sitting on that bluff, just days after watching my ideal future disintegrate in my hands like it was nothing, with the guidance of Merton's words and the ever present invitation of the Spirit, I knew the only thing I had to do was let go.

I had to let go of what I thought I was supposed to be doing for the next five years.

I had to let go of any part of my ego that thought it could gain value from attaining that degree.

I had to let go of any sense of security that came from having a plan.

And I did.

On the spot.

In that exact moment.

So often, we prefer circumstances to be complex and comfortable. But the real work we need to do is usually simple, but painful. And this is always true of letting go.

I let go of the way I thought things were supposed to be, I accepted exactly what they were, which allowed me to open up to the way things could be. I have done this again and again and again throughout my life, because acceptance and letting go are always the journey.

You have to let go of this thing in order to receive the next thing.

You have to stop trying to re-live that moment in order to be able to fully live in this moment.

You have to stop trying to re-create what was in order to create what will be.

Again and again, letting go is the one thing that removes the barriers to the joy we desire, the creativity we carry, and the life God has created us to experience.

If letting go has the power to remove the most fortified barriers to a life of flow, why is letting go the hardest thing we do? Why are we so scared of it? Why does letting go seem to be the one interior movement we resist the most?

Or, why does David Foster Wallace say that, "Everything I've ever let go of has claw marks on it[?]"

And also, what does it mean to let go? What does it feel like to let go? Is it even possible to name and explain the inner mechanism of letting go? Can we practice and get better at the art of letting go?

The modern day mystic Cynthia Bourgeault writes, "Letting go is first and foremost a gesture—a subtle inner drop and release—and every opportunity to practice it strengthens the patterning." With this quote, she initiates us on our journey of answering some of these questions about letting go.

Letting go is felt as an inner drop, as a relaxed release and relinquishing. And yes, one can get better and better at letting go.

But the only way to get better *at* letting go is *by* letting go.

Here are some of my initial thoughts on what letting go is, how it feels, and how it works—think of these thoughts as guiding ideas on the map for the rest of our journey.

Letting go is like a loosening of the clenched muscles in our body that are holding us together, and a surrendering of the defense mechanisms in our mind that are protecting us from pain. It is like a relaxing of our vulnerable heart and a merging of our spirit into the greater love of The Spirit.

Letting go is a sacred handing over.

It feels like a conscious removing of multiple layers of the very clothes that have been covering us for as long as we remember. Followed by a naked and exposed presenting of our selves to the possible presence of a loving God, a benevolent reality, or whatever the hell it is that holds all this together.

And here in this unguarded, undefended, and wide open expanse, we discover for ourselves that grace is all there is, that love is infinitely pouring itself out to the universe, that we are being deeply cared for, and that we truly can be "naked and unashamed."

Letting go can feel like living deeply for the first time.

Also, letting go feels like dying.

Actually, let's take that one step further.

Letting go is dying.

Letting go of something and dying to something are the exact same thing. Which means our resistance to letting go is actually a form of resistance to death. And this doesn't just mean this overarching struggle with the one big death that happens at the end of life, it is more about our refusal to accept the thousands of little deaths that take place during life.

The relationships that end, the seasons that change, the expectations that aren't met, the illusions we have, the plans that fell apart—these are the constant expressions of death we refuse to let go of that end up getting in the way of our life.

This is why Ilia Delio writes, "Only by dying into God can we become one with God, letting go of everything that hinders us from God."

Dying and letting go.

Again and again and again.

Opening up. Letting our guard down. Surrendering.

Again and again and again.

Falling into the Spirit. Merging with God. Being liberated by love.

Again and again and again.

This is what it is to let go. This is the path I am inviting you to trust in your own life.

A little something about me.

I do not ever trust any form of spirituality that does not involve a steady flow of dying and letting go.

Without letting go, you can receive encouragement, you can be taught a more helpful and hopeful vision of life, you will hear cheerleading for your ego, and you will get a management strategy for your false self. But you will never cross that sacred threshold into radical transformation without letting go. A spirituality without death will always remain a first half of life form of faith. It will stay a religion that is empty and impotent in the face of life's greatest problems and God's most powerful invitations.

There is no real liberation without letting go.

With all of that said, I want to be clear that the purpose of this book is to show you that letting go is not simply one thing we do, but rather that which maintains the flow of everything we do.

Each chapter focuses on a specific topic, and names the unique challenges of it and the ways we get stuck within it. Then, shows how some form of letting go is always required in order to do that specific thing well, to sustain joy and peace while doing it, and to become more free as a result of it.

I write with the audacious hope that in each chapter you will see:

Peace requires letting go.

Being present requires letting go.

Joy requires letting go.

Experiencing God and receiving love requires letting go.

Creating requires letting go.

Working for justice requires letting go.

Acceptance requires letting go.

Forgiveness requires letting go.

KEVIN SWEENEY

Growing and evolving requires letting go.

Inclusion requires letting go.

Compassion requires letting go.

The ability to keep going requires letting go.

Owning your inner authority requires letting go

And taking risks requires letting go.

My dream is that everyone who reads this will open up to the possibility that to engage everything from the concrete to the cosmic, from joy to justice, and from the tiniest arguments with your partner to the most monumental social tragedies of our time without losing our joy, we have to learn how to let go.

For some final clarifying words for our journey, my approach to this book and my relationship with letting go are both very simple.

I talk about letting go so much because I have always become more free on the other side of it. I write about dying so casually because it's always a door to new life. I invite people into the darkness so passionately because it is the only place we can see the rays of resurrection light from the future drawing us forward.

And the life changing promise of this book is that if we can keep letting go whenever it is needed, eventually all that is left on the other side is light, and space, and love.

One

BEING PRESENT

It was 2015, and my wife and I were driving through this mesmerizing open space in a Mercedes Sprinter Van in Morocco. We were in Africa for the first time.

Africa.

We had already surfed in Casa Blanca, seen some of the most awe inspiring mosques you can imagine, wandered through the electric streets of Marrakesh, and had just finished driving up and over the Atlas Mountains, the highest point on the entire continent.

We were in Africa.

And in that magical moment—a moment that felt like a dream, a moment that re-grounds you in the mystery of simply being alive—I looked over at this young woman from Pittsburgh and she had out travel books and was researching and planning her next trip somewhere else.

Somewhere else.

We were here, but she was somewhere else.

We were in Morocco, and her mind was already skipping ahead to the next place.

KEVIN SWEENEY

We were in Africa, and she was day dreaming about Sweden or Ibis.

Sometimes it feels like we've mastered everything except the ability to be here.

Your life is happening here. In this moment. Right now. You can read these words trusting and knowing that this is all there is, this is where you will be present to that subtle, yet explosive secret that is quietly hiding in the depths of the obvious.

Life is right here.

This discovery as an embodied experience can transform us into people who truly see our kids, who lose ourselves in what we create, who know the wonder of connection, or who laugh and cry at the miracle of breath. We can wake up, relax the muscles in our face and feel that deep inner uncoiling that allows that subtle smile to form as we rest in the simple feeling of being.

Just this, we say to ourselves as we watch the light dance through the leaves of a tree.

Just this, we know as we take a sip of wine while at dinner with friends.

Just this, we silently shout without any words as we sit across from an unknown friend on the subway.

Being present is the freedom of knowing there is nothing to overcome, nothing to conquer, and nothing that has to be accomplished in order to drink deeply from the endlessly enjoyable mystery of now.

This can sound impossible, it can feel overly simplistic, or maybe even come off as naïve.

I get that.

But it's still true.

One of the three quotes I have on my living room wall comes form the brilliant monk Thich Nhat Hanh, "The miracle is not to walk on water. The miracle is to walk on the green earth in the present moment."

We can believe the miracle that Jesus walked on water, but if we do not become the miracle of waking up and walking in the fullness of the present moment,

what is the point?

I know a lot of people who believe that Jesus walked on water who have almost no access to the wonder of walking in the present. I also know there are people who experience the miracle of the grounding present who do not believe that Jesus literally walked on water. (But that's a different conversation.)

I do not sense the Spirit asking us to look back at that miracle of Jesus, while asking, "Can you believe that miracle and have more faith in God's power?" I actually sense the Spirit asking us to look through the miracle of Christ to right now, while saying, "Can you believe this is a miracle and be more free to be present?"

We should all read that again.

And just in case you are not convinced that either the inability to be present or the ache to be more present are not serious issues for us today, let's look at some of the extreme recreational activities we pursue, or spiritual things we do, and explore why we do them.

Professional surfer and Youtuber, Koa Smith, while describing why he does ice baths (which is exactly what it sounds like, a bath in ice water.) said, "I have so much ideas going through my head, my mind is so loud all the time, I just need something to quiet it."

A former Anglican priest went on a 4 day retreat in the wilderness with only sleeping materials and water. In an interview, he said, "This experience is when silence becomes full for me. It feels like the only space where my mind feels like it flows smoothly."

Surfing legend Greg Long says when he's surfing big waves, distractions are limited, that you can't have drifting thoughts, and how "When I paddle out, it's about being immersed in the water. Everything just sort of dissipates, and in big wave surfing, that happens at a much more heightened level."

One ultra runner describes how ultra marathons require you to be flexible, demand that you consistently let go of your expectations on life, and how "The truth is that the only thing that is ever happening in life is what is happening."

Interesting.

From the thrill of extreme sports, to pursuing grandiose spiritual feats, to the pushing of our bodies to the threshold, and to countless other pursuits in our lives, deep beneath the surface of so much of this extreme activity is the undeniable longing of the human spirit to simply be present.

We want to be here, but we don't know how.

We want to trust in the miracle of the mundane, but we always seem to be somewhere else.

We want to feel completely at home, but like Meister Eckhart said, "God is at home, it is we who have gone out for a walk."

Here is the exciting thing. You do not have to travel to an ashram in India to be awake to the mystery. You do not have to stay in the perfect villa that you saw on Instagram in Bali for a week in order to feel grounded and grateful.

You do not need a month long stay at a temple at the top of the mountain in China to become a part of the unified field.

You do not have to travel any where else, pay for any retreat, or push your body to any extreme in order to be sensitive to the sacred subtleties of the Spirit.

But, you do probably have to do some letting go.

Let's address the obvious question: What does letting go have to do with being present? How can letting go help us be awake and alive to the eternal now? What could we possibly need to let go of in order to smile and rest in the simple feeling of being alive?

Let's answer that with an example. The first thing we have to let go of in order to be present is any form of judgment, need to control, or impulse to change or fix any part of the present.

We have an impossible time being present because we are constantly judging and analyzing the moment. Our natural mode of being is not to love and let the moment be exactly what it is, it is to judge and try to re-organize the moment to become what we think it's supposed to be.

When you need to fix something, you cannot be present.

If you need to change someone, you cannot be present.

When you try and control the moment, you cannot be present.

If your mind cannot accept any specific part of the moment, you cannot be present to the wholeness of the moment. You cannot enjoy the present while your mind is consistently judging the present.

Think about it like this. The less particular you need things to be in order to be present, the more you will be present.

It's actually that simple.

The anxious, particular, and judgmental mind is one of the greatest obstacles to being present.

A friend of mine sat down for a peaceful and relaxing movie with his partner.

(Spoiler alert: The movie ended up being neither peaceful nor relaxing.)

My friend turned the movie on and was ready to sit down and not move for the next couple of hours. His partner had other plans.

While he was sitting, she was standing up and doing other things around the house. While his eyes were completely focused on the movie, her eyes would dart back and forth between the movie and her phone. While he was taking the moment in through stillness, she was taking the moment in through activity.

(How many of you know this life?)

And while this was happening, my friend kept getting more and more frustrated. Which means he was becoming less and less present.

The way she was being during the movie did not fit into my friend's particular vision of how she was supposed to be, or how this moment was supposed to go. Not only was he hoping for a time of connection, but unbeknownst to his conscious mind, he had a specific version of how this connection was supposed to look. And each time her actions did not fit into his version, he became more irritated.

His inability to let go of his expectations got in the way of his experience.

The great activist and mystic, Simone Weil said, "The beautiful is that which we cannot wish to change."

So to be present to and grounded in the beauty of the present, we cannot have a need to change the present.

Or fix the present.

Or control the present.

Or judge the present.

You see how that works? We all want to be present, but there are things within us that we need to let go of in order to be present. The first one is needing to change or control the moment.

It's actually quite simple.

***

The second thing we need to let go of in order to be present is the need to avoid feeling our feelings.

Being unguarded and present will open you up to feel. And the older I get, the more I am convinced that one of the most spiritual things a person can do is to learn how to be present and feel their own feelings.

Through my countless experiences as a pastor and a guide for people on a journey of transformation, one of the most unexpected discoveries I've made is recognizing the ridiculous amount of energy people exert trying to avoid feeling their own feelings.

We can avoid our feelings.

Distract ourselves from our feelings.

Even talk about our feelings.

But we seem to have a deep problem with staying still and actually feeling our feelings.

The great Ken Wilber said, "We will do anything except come to rest in the pure Presence of the present." Maybe this is because in order to be open and unguarded to the present means we have to be open and welcoming to our feelings.

Whether we are aware of it or not, we can be afraid of being present.

Before you jump to the conclusion that either of these claims are ridiculous, let's take a look at an experiment that was published in *Science,* in 2014. In this experiment, participants were left alone in a room for fifteen minutes.

No phone, no books, no stimuli at all.

Just them.

After the fifteen minutes, over half of the participants stated that they did not like or enjoy spending the time alone.

In later stages of the experimentation, the participants were shocked with an electric device. Now, this shock was so uncomfortable that the majority of the receivers of the shock said they would pay money to ensure that they would not be shocked again.

(Stay with me. This is going somewhere.)

The final part of the experiment left these same people alone for another fifteen minutes, only this time the researchers left the electric device in there with them. And the shocking discovery they made (I had to), was that over half of the men, and about twenty five percent of the women chose to shock themselves during that time alone.

They deliberately decided to introduce physical pain into their lives while in silence.

Do you see what was happening?

They chose to inflict physical pain on themselves instead of being present.

While being provided a space to be alone with and present to their life, they chose a painful distraction.

They literally chose physical pain over presence.

So, am I saying that this experiment proves conclusively that we avoid being present because we are afraid to feel our feelings? No. But I do believe it raises all kinds of interesting questions about what it is that is so uncomfortable about simply being, that would make such a high percentage of people choose physical discomfort as an alternative.

Being present requires us to be open and engaged enough to feel, and I suspect that flowing through the kinetic energy of so much of our lives is this hidden and mysterious resistance to feeling whatever it is that is there.

Yes, being present will draw to the surface uncomfortable feelings that have been lingering inside of us. And while our initial mindless reaction is often to bypass these emotions, it is the facing and feeling of these emotions as they arise that helps create so much of the space to actually be present.

When Rumi writes, "The moment you accept what troubles you've been given, the door will open[,]" we see that the door he is referring to is one that allows us to feel welcome in the home of the present. And in order to walk through this door and feel home, we have to learn how to become comfortable with feeling.

Another thing we need to let go of in order to be present is the need to cling to any particular moment. A hidden force that can pull us away from the present is our struggle to accept the passing nature of our experiences. As we begin to settle into the goodness and beauty of the present, something within us is reminded that it is not going to last, and this reminder can create a sense of fear.

Fear of loss.

Fear that happiness is not going to last.

Fear that it may never get this good again.

And this fear of losing the moment makes it impossible to simply the love the moment. Our worry that we're never going to get the beauty back strips us of the power to receive it in the first place.

One of the coolest things about being married or having a long term partner is the amount of running inside jokes you have. Sometimes they're expressed through facial expressions or noises, other times they're shared by phrases only you both understand.

"Of course!"

"Hmmmmmm, yeah, thats tough babe."

"You're great!"

These are some of the inside joke phrases in our marriage. Now that I think about it, I'm actually the only one whoever says these things in our marriage. I think my wife just lovingly gives me the space to say them over and over so I can entertain myself.

And one of the longest running ongoing jokes my wife and I have is this idea of "once a month."

Since we were in our early twenties, almost any time we would be out and Christine would be having a great time, she would inevitably turn to me at some point in the night and say, "Can we do this once a month?"

Once a month.

So funny.

To make sense of this, you need to understand that there were two things at work within her whenever she would say this: (1) she was tuned in to the sacredness of the moment; and (2) she would feel a sense of fear that we were never going to get this moment back.

So even now—fifteen years later—whenever I know she's having an amazing time, I'll turn to her and say jokingly, "Once a month?"

Here's the thing.

Her fear isn't losing the particular arrangement of life in the moment, it's losing the depth, the beauty, and the goodness within the moment. Our fear of loss when we are enjoying the present actually has nothing to do with the form of the circumstances, it has to do with our fear of never getting back the substance of life we experience through the circumstances.

We experience the miracle of the moment, and we're scared of losing the moment because we think the miracle goes with it.

Which is why Rumi says, "Don't grieve. Anything you lose comes round in another form."

So what do we need to let go of in order to be present? Our fear that life is never going to be this good again.

The Spirit invites us to trust that the foundational goodness of life transcends any specific arrangement of reality, while remaining fully present within each one at the same time.

The last thing that I will mention that needs to be let go of in order to be present is the need to be productive. No matter how many different ways this is said, the part of our ego that feels the constant compulsion to produce, to perform, or to get ahead is going to keep trying to force us into the future and out of the present moment.

If you need to perform, being present provides no audience.

If you need to produce, the present is experienced as empty.

If you need to get ahead, being present is viewed as falling behind.

I was thirty-two years old when my daughter was in the first year of her life. While my wife and I were leading our church, she was also working as a therapist at the time. So, every single day, I would be with our daughter solo for about three hours.

This is the stage of life where you learn how unbelievably exhausted one tiny little human can make you.

I remember one day while it was just my daughter and I. We were in our little front yard playing with the hose, surrounded by water toys, and just sort of sitting there and rolling around in the grass. And at some point during that instance, I thought about how much other people who are in my vocational sphere were doing to get ahead. I thought of how hard they could be working to build their churches, to make a name for themselves, or now as I look back, how much energy they were exerting building their platforms.

(Building your platform. I can't even begin to go there right now.)

These thoughts, and the concerns of my ego about falling behind prevented me from being present to the miracle of my daughter. Thinking about what others were doing to get ahead pulled me away from my daughter who was right there. The constant need to produce or compete becomes one of the greatest obstacles to the present.

And as these thoughts began to arise, I recognized them, I allowed them their space, and I observed and acknowledged them. In that moment, I had to accept the truth that being present to my daughter did nothing for my platform, did not further my name, and did not help with any kind of networking.

Being present does not help you build a platform.

But as I sat with all of this, saw it with great clarity, and surrendered and let go of any need to produce, to compete, or to attempt to keep up with others, I returned to my daughter with tears in my eyes, the sun on my face, and grass on my feet and continued doing nothing with her.

Being awake and alive to my daughter demanded that I let go.

(And often times, as a follower of Jesus, it is an ironic form of letting go. Our letting go can be ironic because what you are letting go of is the obsessive grind that gives you the kind of platform to talk about the kind of life that is only experienced if you let go of the need for the public platform or position in the first place.)

In the end, letting go gives you nothing.

And within that experience of nothing, you receive everything.

Two

BEGINNING AGAIN

On the very first Easter morning in human history, Jesus appeared to two of his disciples and began to walk with them on this long road to Emmaus. Now, from our historical and religious vantage point, we can see that this was a new morning, that this was the day creation had been waiting for, that this was the turning point in cosmic history.

This was resurrection.

But since the disciples were not aware of resurrection, for them it was a day where all of their dreams had died, their expectations had been shattered, and as a result, a day they had lost all hope.

The gospel of Luke says, their "faces [were] downcast" (v.17) because they "had hoped he was the one who was going to redeem Israel…" and he didn't.

Jesus was supposed to save them, redeem them, and put them back in power and make everything right. Instead, they saw their leader get killed, they felt they were not safe, and it was all over.

They thought their life was going to go one way, and it did not go the way they hoped or planned for.

Have you ever had that experience? Have you ever watched the blueprint for your future disappear? Have you ever been so sure of a plan for your life, only to eventually witness it die right in front of you?

Of course.

It's called your 20s.

And especially your 30s.

And if the pattern holds, I'm assuming your 40s too.

In some of the early and defining chapters of our lives, the questions around vocation are: Are you going to have the courage to offer your gifts and passions to this world? Are you going to take the necessary risks to give your life wholeheartedly? Are you going to dare to pour your life out as the sacred offering that is?

Which means the deeper question in these early stages is,

are you going to begin?

But when you say yes to this, and take those daring first steps, eventually you will travel far enough to see that the defining questions change. After we struggle, face challenges, are confronted with heart break, get crushed by betrayal, witness relationships end, and are forced to watch seasons change, a different set of decisive questions emerge.

Are you going to keep saying yes to this courageous journey? Can you keep going? Are you still going to choose to try, to care, and to keep showing up? Are you going to dare to rise again even though the last fall felt like the end?

Now, the question is not, are you going to begin? The real question becomes,

are you going to begin again?

And again?

And again?

And again?

When I was in graduate school, it was my dream to be able to teach at a Christian College one day (funny how things change). And during this chapter of my education, I attended an academic conference in San Francisco called The American Academy of Religion. Or AAR.

It's basically Comic Con for theology nerds.

But instead of waiting in line to take a picture with Loki, you sit in a poorly lit room and listen to a professor no one else has ever heard of talk about something most people don't care about.

And I had a great time.

Over the course of a few days, I had a meeting with one of the heads of a college in Hawaii. I shared with him my dreams and plans of moving back to the islands in a couple years. We connected very naturally, and eventually he offered me a job teaching after I finished my degrees.

Everything was coming together, my dreams were coming true, and one of my ultimate aspirations was coming to fruition at such an organic pace. So I finished grad school, moved to back to Hawaii six months later, started teaching at the school, and was so excited.

And after one semester, I was essentially let go and eventually banned from campus.

(I wish you could see how much I was laughing as I wrote that.)

The details of what happened are not important for here, but let's just say I know a little something about having expectations shattered.

Months later, I remember waking up early to work on a lecture about being creative and prophetic because a good friend of mine and teacher at the school asked me to come and teach his class for a day (this was before I was banned but after I was let go).

I was tired from people being at our house late at night after church, but I was also eager to be back in class teaching with the students.

After a less than warm welcome on campus one time after I got let go, I texted my friend on the way to double check that he cleared my time there with one of the deans. He asked if I was serious, and I responded with a yes, and told him he should check.

A few minutes later my friend called me with a great sense of sincerity in his voice, and he told me he was so sorry, but the dean said I was not allowed to come on campus and teach. I told him I understood, that it wasn't on him, and that it was all good with us.

Wow.

Excluded from the one place I dreamt of being.

Banned from an environment that I believed I was meant to be.

Rejected by the people who I hoped would be guides for me.

I hung up the phone, did an extremely illegal u-turn in the middle of the street right in front of a Jack in the Box, and drove back to my house in that heavy silence that feels like you're wearing a weighted jacket. I got home, laid down on my couch and had trouble getting up from it for the next few hours.

I was hurt.

The people I counted on crushed me.

I was in disbelief, disillusioned, wondering what the hell just happened.

And I know you have been hurt too.

I bet you have had people you have counted on crush you too.

I assume you have had to sit in those heavy spaces feeling and wondering the exact same thing.

In these dark and defining times, we so desperately wish that life could only be light. We become filled with this primal rage against the inescapable pain and suffering of life that our ego so cleverly tries to out maneuver. We angrily tip toe along that fine line between hard and holy, refusing to accept that there actually is no line at all.

We wish it didn't have to be so hard.

Yes. Yes. Yes to all of that.

But still, the brilliant visionary Mirabai Starr says that "It's that keeping the heart open, even in hell, that makes space for the Beloved."

Yes. Yes. Yes to all of that too.

Our greatest hurts can become the wombs for our greatest hopes. Like the Holy Saturday between the death of Jesus and the resurrection of Christ, those painful, dark, uncertain in-between spaces can be transformed into light and liberation.

But in order for that beautiful and gut wrenching transfiguration to happen, there is probably something hard we need to accept about where we are, and deeply painful we have to let go of in order to keep going and begin again.

Let's go back to the Easter story of Jesus walking with his disciples. Remember, these are people who are hurting and struggling to make sense of their life because their expectations have been shattered and their old story of how life was supposed to go fell apart.

They are carrying pain, confusion, bewilderment, and are having a hard time seeing the way forward.

In Luke 24, after first appearing to the disciples, Jesus now re-tells the ancient story of Scripture through Him, and then sits down at dinner with them.

Jesus "Explained to them what was said in the Scriptures concerning himself." (V. 25-27)

Jesus "Broke the bread and gave it to them…and their eyes were opened." (V. 30-32)

Jesus asked "Why are you troubled…look at my hands and my feet." (V. 37-39)

This is the crucified and resurrected Jesus with marks on his hands to prove he had gone to the limit and crossed over the threshold of pain, evil, and death itself, now present as the unstoppable divine life force he always was. He put his scars on display as a way of showing the seamless reality of death and resurrection.

He had scars, but He was still there.

So when the grief and weight of reality was met by, embraced through, and overcome in Jesus, a path opened up for this same experience to become true in us as well. Jesus overcame suffering, which means we can as well. Jesus' life extended beyond death, and that means our life extends beyond any form of death too.

Resurrection was the deepest truth expressed in Jesus, and it can become the greatest truth experienced by us.

In light of this, what does letting go have to do with overcoming pain, disappointment, and beginning again? Why would we need to let go in order to keep going? What do we need to let go of in order to move beyond suffering and return to the sacred vocation of our lives?

The first and one of the most central things we have to learn to let go of in order to keep going is expectations.

Letting go of expectations liberates us to begin again.

"Okay," you say.

Well...what expectations are you talking about? I mean, some expectations are necessary right? Which expectations are we supposed to let go of?

All of them.

Every single one.

No exceptions.

You relinquish and release every individual expectation you have on work, relationships, and God until you can finally let go of expectation itself.

On Good Friday, every single expectation the disciples had on Jesus was crucified, buried, and died with Jesus. And only after all of these false and dangerous expectations had been buried, was Jesus able to return to them in the power of resurrection and say,

let's keep going.

Resurrection bursts forth in our life whenever we are ready. And we transcend the gridlock of our imagination and become ready by letting go of any and all expectations that were keeping us stuck in the first place.

Expectations always get in the way of the future the Spirit is inviting you into.

In the depth of our most frustrating, discouraging, and disappointing moments, it isn't just the presence of pain that creates struggle, it is the exposing of the power of our expectations by the present pain that becomes the hardest part of the struggle.

Painful experiences in life carry the power to expose our expectations on life.

The hard to shake frustration with those particular people not showing up for you when you counted on them exposes your expectation that people that you support are always supposed to support you in the same way (Which they won't).

The envy and anger you feel about that one person's (who you know is willing to compromise their integrity and character to get ahead) success exposes your expectation that life is somehow supposed to be fair (Which it's not).

The resentment you have toward that group of friends and collaborators who seem to have everything, exposes your expectations that you're supposed to be a part of a group just like that (Which you aren't).

You see how that works?

Every disappointing experience we have in life can expose an expectation we have on life.

Which is so important because the painful experience hurts for the moment, the expectations you have hinder you for a lifetime.

The concrete experience confronts our expectations, and draws them closer to the surface of our life. Of course it is painful. But this exposing carries so much potential because it is only the naming and letting go of these expectations that has the power to free us from the frustration that is making it feel so impossible to keep going or begin again.

I remember a heavier season in my life and the life of our church, where the main prayer I would pray to God was,

"What the fuck?"

Yes. You read that correctly.

No. That is not somewhere in the psalms.

(Although, I do feel that energy within quite a bit of the psalms. I mean, the psalmist did pray to God that the heads of his enemies' babies would be smashed on rocks. So, who really has the issues here?)

Actually sometimes I would grimace and groan that prayer in a time of silence, and actually say with tears in my eyes, "what the fuck man?"

Which is hilarious, because it sounded like I was sixteen years old and upset with one of my stoner buddies.

But that prayer was born out of a time where I was being confronted by the loss of relationships I previously cherished and felt supported by. Where I was seeing and experiencing the intensity of pressure and tension that starting and leading a church together puts on a marriage. It came out of a season where the financial sacrifices we made to have the freedom to build a church we believed in were making it impossible to see anything on the horizon that was going to make our life actually work.

It was the prayer of pain and impossibility.

And yet, within that prayer was the letting go of and the overcoming of certain expectations.

A part of me thought that the people you love deeply are always going to love you back.

No. I needed to let go of that.

A part of me assumed when you are taking this many risks and living with this much trust in God for the sake of others, it shouldn't be this hard on a marriage.

Nope. I needed to let go of that too.

During those times in silence with God where I would feel, grieve, and name everything I needed to let go of in order to keep going, that irreverent prayer was actually the most reverent thing I could do. That tear soaked question and prayer was a part of me accepting how painful it was to let go of the expectations I had on how pastoring was supposed to feel. It was also a prayer of letting go and entrusting my life to God.

Which is why the brilliant Mirabai Starr says, "We know how to enter the heart of every kind of suffering and stay with it until it gives way to any kind of awakening."

One hundred percent yes.

Suffering and awakening. Suffering and awakening. Suffering and awakening.

And this path from suffering to awakening is made possible by letting go.

Every single time.

As we return to that Easter morning one more time, we can still hear this subtle invitation from Christ today through his ancient re-telling of this story. The gospel writer writes,

Then he opened their minds so they could understand the Scriptures. He told them, "This is what is written: The Messiah will suffer and rise from the dead on the third day…" (v.45-46)

What is at the heart of the ancient story Jesus is telling?

The Messiah will suffer *and* rise.

Suffering and rising.

Not a radical path of love without being crucified, suffering and rising.

Not a non-stop upward trajectory to heaven, suffering and rising.

Not the depth of joy without the presence of pain, suffering and rising.

If we want to become the same kind of unstoppable divine life force as Jesus, a person who is not only able to keep going, but who is able to keep their heart open and filled with joy while they keep going, there is some serious letting go we need to do.

And in order to begin again, we have to let go of the need to avoid pain, death, and suffering.

The French mystic Jeanne Guyon said "It is only by the death of self that the soul can enter into Divine Truth, and understand in part what is the light that shineth in darkness."

This resistance to pain, this need to reject suffering, this primal avoidance of any form of death are some of our greatest barriers to keeping our heart open and beginning again.

When we feel the most hurt and stuck, and are left wondering if we can keep going, so often, what we are truly saying is,

"I don't think I can deal with any more loss."

"I cannot face anymore heartbreak."

"I'm not ready to hear any more criticism."

"I can't accept the hard parts of this work anymore."

I hear all of that. I know all of that. I have lived and still live all of that.

But also, and I write this with a real sense of compassion, until we are able to let go of that part of our separate self that still needs to avoid hurt and pain in order to keep doing our sacred work in this world, we will never be free to live a life of resurrection.

We so desperately want the world to be split into two.

Joy or pain.

Life or death.

Crucifixion or resurrection

Good or bad.

But when Jesus returned to the disciples and to our world with his scars, He is showing how what they perceive as separate experiences of suffering and joy are a part of the same flow. He is re-connecting life and death and disclosing their link as seamless stages of one single journey. He is revealing crucifixion and resurrection as two inseparable steps on the unified path of incarnation. He is holding together and breaking down every single relationship of opposites we struggle to put together in his own crucified AND resurrected body.

He is taking two and making it one.

Now, its

Joy and pain.

Life and death.

Crucifixion and resurrection

Good and bad.

We have to learn how to hold these relationships of opposites together in our own bodies the same way Jesus did.

And we do this by acceptance and letting go.

And once we start to do this, we directly realize the truth of the experience Ken Wilber was referring to when he said "You don't recoil from death or grasp at life, since fundamentally they are both just simple experiences that pass."

Accepting pain, and embracing suffering is one of the ultimate forms of letting go. When you do this,

You no longer get surprised by pain.

You have no need to keep suffering at a distance when it arises within you.

And you do not spend your life trying to avoid the hard parts and clinging to the holy parts because the lines between hard and holy have been dissolved in the center of the Christ within your own being. And like Jesus, you keep returning to love and you keep beginning again because you've already accepted in the depths of your life that the real journey is always suffering and rising.

This why Starr reminds us that "Christ's evolution of Spirit between abandonment and reunion serves as a model for the universal process of opening the heart, despite every reason not to."

Opening the heart.

Despite every reason not to.

Yes. Damnit. Damnit. Damnit. But yes.

Just recently, our core team of friends who help lead our church Imagine together were planning what the next couple of months would look like for our church as we prepare to re-open everything up after Covid restrictions. After talking about a small group of twelve people we were going to focus much of our creative energy guiding into this new chapter, one of my friends in our group said,

"I have to be honest, thinking about doing this and opening my heart again is making my stomach feel like it has knots in it."

My wife replied,

"Me too. I'm with you girl."

My wife and my friend both had feelings of fear or worry because of the possibility of pain, relational loss, and hard times with people.

And of course, I understand these feelings, and have these thoughts as well. Within these comments are past experiences of trauma, vivid memories of hurt, and the fear of having these forms of pain re-enter our lives.

This is the disciples after the crucifixion.

This is you after the hardest seasons of your life.

This was our team after everything we've been through.

This is why we always somehow return to these questions. Can we open our heart up again? Can we really keep going? Can we truly begin again?

Yes.

We can.

We keep flinging the doors of our heart wide open until the day they stay open permanently. Or as the great Sufi Inayat Khan said, we embrace and accept that "God breaks the heart again and again until it stays open."

Letting go allows us to stay open, remain unguarded, and to finally remain free

to begin again,

and again,

and again,

despite every reason we have not to.

Three

COMPASSION

Our church leads something called The Jesus Dojo.

The Jesus Dojo.

How great is that?

While I would love to be able to take credit for the name and concept, I can't. This experience is inspired by Mark Scandrette, who is the creator of The Jesus Dojo in San Francisco.

For us, the Jesus Dojo is a six week journey practicing and living the ways of Jesus. It is not a classroom environment where we simply learn about Jesus, it is an experiential and embodied path where we actually do the things Jesus did, live the life Jesus discussed, and become the things we claim to believe. We practice hospitality, extending forgiveness, sharing and carrying each other's burdens, praying in the city, and practicing compassion toward the marginalized in our neighborhood.

For the compassion experience, I take the group to a shelter in our neighborhood we have had a relationship with for a long time. When the people go to the shelter, they are not able to bring anything but their presence.

No blankets.

KEVIN SWEENEY

No sandwiches.

No material goods of any kind.

Nothing to offer except their own presence.

We do this because bringing something to give and offering something tangible can function as a security blanket that covers the vulnerability of offering our presence alone. Sometimes beginning by having something to offer places the giver in a power position that protects them from the kind of mutual vulnerability and openness that is required for real relationship.

So bringing nothing except your presence creates an environment of mutual vulnerability, the possibility for real connection, and a space for genuine compassion to arise.

Henri Nouwen said, "Too many churches try to provide cures before they've learned to care."

It is too easy to give people things without loving them, and to help people without ever knowing them. And stripping people of these distance creating "gifts" brings them deeper into the life of the place, and the lives of the people.

Or at least that's the hope.

Through the years of taking different groups into the shelter, I've realized what a new and shocking experience it is for so many. Some people have never seen an entire family living in what looks like a small cubby. It could be their first time hearing stories of how people ended up in the streets, or being close to the journey of someone who feels lost and stuck in a shelter. It might even be their first time ever actually speaking to someone homeless.

This can feel like an alarm clock waking them up to the truth of suffering in the same neighborhood with all of the new condos, boutiques and restaurants they love.

This experience can make people feel

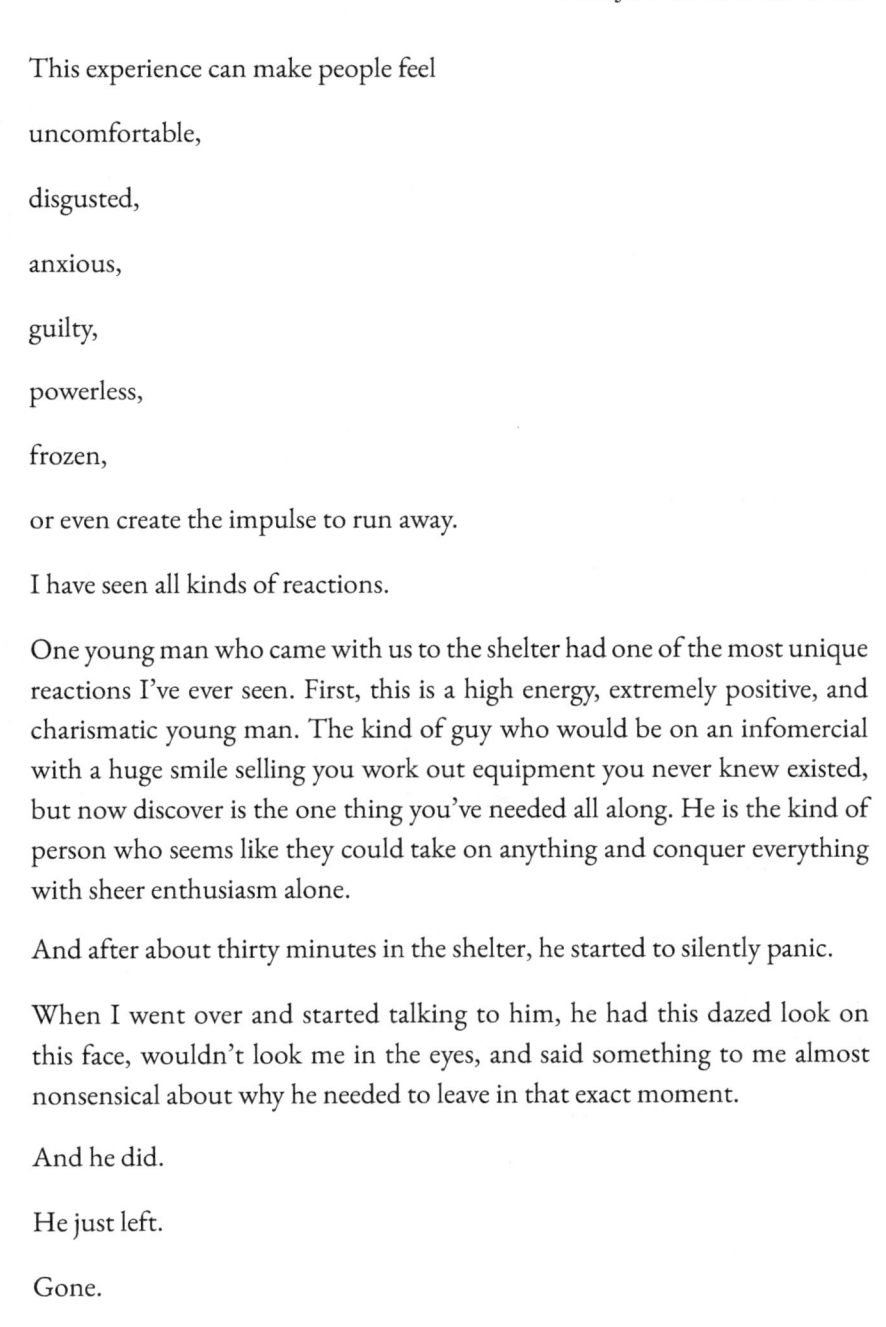

uncomfortable,

disgusted,

anxious,

guilty,

powerless,

frozen,

or even create the impulse to run away.

I have seen all kinds of reactions.

One young man who came with us to the shelter had one of the most unique reactions I've ever seen. First, this is a high energy, extremely positive, and charismatic young man. The kind of guy who would be on an infomercial with a huge smile selling you work out equipment you never knew existed, but now discover is the one thing you've needed all along. He is the kind of person who seems like they could take on anything and conquer everything with sheer enthusiasm alone.

And after about thirty minutes in the shelter, he started to silently panic.

When I went over and started talking to him, he had this dazed look on this face, wouldn't look me in the eyes, and said something to me almost nonsensical about why he needed to leave in that exact moment.

And he did.

He just left.

Gone.

There was something about witnessing the hard realities in that shelter that made it impossible for him to be present, which of course makes it impossible to have compassion. The atmosphere of suffering and struggle had enough power that it rendered one of the most seemingly powerful people virtually lifeless and unable to simply be.

Fascinating.

I wonder what was going on there.

In Matthew 9:36, Jesus is walking amongst a mass of people, and the text says, "When he saw the crowds, he had compassion on them, because they were harassed and helpless, like sheep without a shepherd."

The word compassion here comes from the Greek word *splagchnnon*, which means,

the kidneys,

center of your being,

to be moved in your inward parts,

the seat of your affections,

and is connected to the Hebrew word for womb.

So for Jesus to have compassion on people means he felt deeply and was moved in the depths of his center in a way that gave birth to action.

Jesus reveals something essential about the nature of compassion and what it demands of us.

Compassion requires us to feel.

The Celtic mystic John Phillip Newell writes, "Compassionate action is sustained by the courage to feel." Newell builds on this by showing that a continuous life of compassion is held together by a perpetual commitment to feel.

The word compassion literally means "to suffer with," or to just be with suffering.

If real compassion demands that we hold space long enough to feel the suffering heart of another, perhaps that young man in the shelter was confronted by feelings and emotions that were too much to handle. That environment of struggle and pain kept knocking on the door of his heart trying to get him to welcome it in, but for some reason, that emotional gamble was too much of a risk for him to take.

The invitation of compassion was asking him to feel something he wasn't ready to feel.

Later on, when we finally discussed that day, he told me exactly what he was feeling. He told me that as a young man growing up how he did, he knew with just a few bad decisions and a tough season, he could easily end up in a place like that. Their poverty viscerally confronted him with his fear of his own possible poverty.

He couldn't accept their suffering into him because it scared him, and required him to feel one of his greatest fears—ending up poor or in a shelter himself.

To be a person of compassion, we need to have the courage to feel.

Think about these questions.

Why do we crack jokes or make sarcastic comments when someone is expressing deep hurt?

Why do we get anxious and get this impulse to flee when someone is being vulnerable?

Why do we feel so uncomfortable when one person is deeply comforting another person in our presence?

Why does a part of us get angry and want to tell the person to get over it when they're allowing themselves to be "weak?"

Maybe it's because if we don't do these things and remain present, it means we will remain open. And if we remain open, we will have to feel something we don't want to feel. This concept is echoed by the great Henri Nouwen when he says "Compassion requires us to be weak with the weak, vulnerable with the vulnerable, and powerless with the powerless."

Real compassion dismantles us, disassembles us, and invites us to entrust whatever feelings arise to the Spirit that always transcends our own capacity to hold ourselves together.

If compassion requires feeling things we are uncomfortable feeling, what is it we might have to feel in order remain present enough to extend compassion?

Which actually brings us back to the ongoing question about letting go.

What needs to be let go of in order to have compassion?

To begin with some honesty.

One of the deepest things we need to let go of in order to be compassionate is the avoidance of feeling powerless and helpless.

In 2013, Christine and I moved back to Oahu from Costa Mesa, CA, where we lived for about five years after getting married. We were both done with graduate school, came to the end of our chapter in Orange County, and had begun this new adventure of moving back to the Hawaii to start a church.

We stepped beyond the exciting and thrilling stage of imagination, where you dream and dare to see possibilities beyond your current horizon, and into the challenging stage of implementation.

We were now officially doing it.

And for the first two weeks of living out this new quest, that meant sleeping on the floor of an empty house because all of the furniture we had shipped from Long Beach hadn't arrived yet.

No pillows. No blankets. No cozy mattress. Just the floor, each other, and a mutual movement toward what felt like the abyss of the unknown.

'Til death do us part baby!

I remember one of the first long nights in that house, Christine woke me up multiple times because it was cold and she wanted something to cover her. (And by cold during winter time in Hawai'i, I mean it was probably 75 degrees.)

Each time I would get up, grab a few random pieces of clothing from her suitcase and strategically place them on top of her to try and keep her warm. After a few more nudges of waking me up throughout the night, I finally stood up and just emptied the whole suitcase on her!

I've always been a romantic.

But those dark nights were more than just the discomfort of the empty house. It was the intensity of looking into the void of the unknown, the feeling of being enveloped by the uncertainty of the future, and the ongoing conversation with doubt about the complete upending of our life.

Many of those first nights, Christine would cry herself to sleep as she exhaustively expressed every fear, regret, and doubt about the decision we just made. And as she went down the list of why what we were doing was a huge mistake, or told me how desperately she wanted to go home, I could feel my ego contracting so intensely as I was tempted to aggressively explain to her why this wasn't just my fault. I kept feeling this part of me that wanted defend itself by reminding her how we both made this decision together.

"You were the one who was so excited every time we told people what we were doing."

"This is what you wanted too!"

"Stop complaining and crying about the reality that you helped create."

But, I didn't say any of those things. (Especially glad I did not say the last one!)

Instead, I just lay there next to her. I was present to her, and took all of her fear, all of her pain, and all of her suffering into my body and just let it be. And when I did,

I felt helpless.

I felt disarmed.

I felt powerless.

I could not take away her fear. I wasn't able to explain the pain out of her. I could not fix the struggle of the moment.

Those unbearably heavy spaces where the people you love the most are hurting and you cannot do anything to change it or make it stop—that feeling of powerlessness is something you have to accept in order to be a grounding presence of compassion. And during those gut wrenching nights, surrendering the need to fix the situation was made possible through me welcoming the intensity of uncomfortable feelings into my body.

This is where we learn to move from fixing to feeling.

Desmond Tutu, in his brilliant book with The Dali Lama, *The Book of Joy*, said, "We fear compassion because we're afraid of experiencing suffering, the vulnerability, and the helplessness that can come with having an open heart."

We have to let go of the need to avoid that form of helplessness and powerlessness to become a space of compassion. If we are unable to let go of this need to avoid these experiences, we will always be explaining, justifying, blaming, getting angry, or deflecting as a way of distracting ourselves from the feelings that arise in the furnace of compassion.

The part of me that wanted to explain the situation, justify our circumstances, or place blame back on Christine was just my ego needing to defend itself from that foundational experience of powerlessness that we seem to avoid like it is death itself.

Which makes sense, since powerlessness is a form of death. And also why the mystic, Seraphim of Sarov said, "Silence is the cross on which we must crucify our ego."

Accepting powerlessness is:

The death of the illusion that you are in control.

The death of the ego's need to prevent our loved ones from feeling pain.

The death of the belief that we are responsible for anyone else's emotions.

And the death of the idea that if someone we love is hurting, we are the ones to blame.

Being compassionate always means something within us needs to die.

Compassion insists that we let go of our avoidance of powerlessness, and invites us to entrust the ones we love to the power of God. Compassion says, it's okay to just be here with your unarmed presence and your unguarded heart, and simply be close. Compassion teaches us that we do not have to personalize anyone else's pain, feel guilty for it, or feel less valuable because of it.

Being present to the suffering of others does not take anything away from our essential Self.

This is where we discover the power of powerlessness, and understand why the apostle Paul, said, "When I am weak, then I am strong."

Only when we let go of the power to be productive for someone, are we able to be compassionate with someone.

Surrendering the impulse to avoid powerlessness mysteriously awakens us to live from the power of God. Resisting the urge to speak, allows our silence to become the very place where only the Spirit can speak. Being compassionate by letting go of our need to avoid powerlessness allows both the other and ourselves to awaken to the power that comes directly from God.

Second, with the aim of becoming people of compassion, we need to let go of the need to change or save anyone.

You cannot fix anyone else.

You cannot change anyone else.

You cannot save anyone else.

And when you try, you are stifling the other person, and suffocating yourself.

(By the way, I just saved you three years of therapy.)

Compassion calls us to move beyond the need to explain suffering to someone, so we're finally free to experience suffering with someone. This is the daring summons of the compassionate way. We do not need to change another person or get them to see why they shouldn't be hurt in the first place. We simply need to bear witness to the pain, and stay present enough to see them with the affirmative gaze of God while they are afflicted.

When I finally let go of the need to change you, I am now free to love you.

You want to know something?

It is dangerous to worship Jesus' journey from a distance without walking Jesus' journey closely. Too often, people only want Jesus because he promises them heaven, when what Christ wants is to walk with us through hell.

Which is why every year for Good Friday, our church journeyed through the stations of the cross together through personal storytelling and music. We do this by reading one of the stations of the cross, offering a brief explanation of what was happening, having someone share a personal story of experiencing what Jesus did in that moment, singing a repetitive chorus together, and then repeating that pattern.

It creates this powerful and entrancing flow.

So when we read about one of Jesus' experiences of humiliation, someone comes to the front and shares their story of humiliation.

When we read about one of Jesus's experiences of betrayal, someone comes to the front and tells a story of when they were betrayed.

When we read about one of Jesus's stories about being abandoned, someone comes to the front and tells a story of when they were abandoned.

Over the years,

We have heard stories of sexual assault.

We have heard stories of fathers who never stuck around.

We even heard a story from a young person who feared rejection for being LGBTQ, while actually coming out to the church in that same moment.

And after each gut wrenching story, there is no encouraging word, no Bible verse given to make things better, no attempt to ease our own discomfort or bypass the person's suffering—just silent solidarity and compassion, and us singing together.

This hour and half long journey allows everyone who is attending to practice real compassion, because the only way to be present in this context is to remain silent.

Many people from Imagine say this is their favorite gathering of the entire year. They talk about how this experience is heavy and intense, and holy and healing at the same time.

How can that be possible? Why would a night where we remember the death, humiliation, and suffering of Jesus somehow be people's favorite time of the year?

I assume it has to do with the power of compassion.

On that night, the community collectively holds that awkward and unbearable space that emerges while sitting in the presence of depth and suffering.

THE JOY OF LETTING GO

And at the same time, by letting go of the urge to explain it, fix it, or change it, allows the healing power of the Spirit enough space to breathe through us as a whole.

Justin Rosenstein, the guy who created the like button for Facebook, purchased a new iPhone and instructed his assistant to set up a parental-control feature to prevent him from downloading any apps. He also banned himself from snapchat. Rosenstein says everyone is distracted all the time

Leah Pearlman, who was on the original design team for the like feature on Facebook, has installed a web browser plug-in to eradicate her Facebook news feed, and hired a social media manager to monitor her Facebook page so that she doesn't have to.

Loren Brichter, the guy who invented the pull/refresh feature regrets it: he regrets it because he thinks people are addicted to their phones, always on, completely distracted, and unable to live in the moment.

These tech innovators are weaning themselves off of their own products because of how impossible it makes it to ever be fully present in our lives.

Sometimes it seems like we are interested in being anywhere other than where we are. We're in this moment remembering that moment, or in this moment looking forward to the next moment. We are talking and scrolling, watching and shopping, we're always here and there, but never wholly in either. It is so easy to live with a continuous "partial attention."

We live in a culture where we are hyperconnected and easily distracted, and always available but rarely present.

So, what does any of this have to do with compassion?

You cannot be compassionate to people you cannot see. And in order to see people with the eyes of compassion, we have to let go of a life of constant distraction.

The Nobel Peace Prize recipient, Aung San Suu Kyi's three-fold path of compassion is the courage to see, the courage to feel, and the courage to act. While most of this chapter is about sustaining the courage to feel in order to be compassionate, Suu Kyi reveals an even more essential part of the compassionate way, which is seeing.

Remember the story of Jesus in Matthew 9:36?

The Scriptures say, "When he saw the crowds, he had compassion on them, because they were harassed and helpless, like sheep without a shepherd."

He saw the crowds.

Before anything else, Jesus saw people.

Jesus was awake and undistracted enough to see.

You can only include someone in a deep enough way to have compassion on them and to feel their life when you are not distracted. You can only experience the depth of another person when you are not distracted. You can only truly love another person when you are not distracted, and able to see them and be present to them.

Jesus seems to have had the skill of living totally in the now, giving undivided attention to the present task, and being fully engaged with whatever was in front of him. Jesus' capacity to be present, and his ability to truly see was one of the defining marks of his life.

You cannot be distracted and compassionate at the same time.

This is why one of the most practical things we need to let go of in order to become compassionate is the pace of life that prevents us from seeing. If we're honest, many of us are just too busy to see others deeply. But the compassionate way calls us beyond the intensity and distractions into the simplicity of seeing—because this is where compassion is born.

Compassion insists that we have the courage to feel.

Compassion invites us to let go of our need to change or save anyone else.

Compassion is born out of our ability to see people.

The great mystic Hildegarde of Bingen said, "God hugs you. You are encircled by the arms of the mystery of God."

And if we can let go enough to daringly embrace this life of compassion, we can become those very arms that extend this mystery of God into our world.

Four

EXPERIENCING GOD AND RECEIVING LOVE

We love good quotes don't we?

We listen to podcasts, teachings, interviews, or sermons, and are always so primed for a great one liner to be shared. And when it finally comes, our anticipation of and excitement for the moment meet and are usually followed by an agreeable noise or phrase.

"Hmmmm....."

"Wow."

"So good."

"Yes."

Or sometimes even a good, "Damn." (Thats pronounced more like "dayuu uum.")

The truth of a single statement carries so much profundity as it connects with the state of our current existence that we have to react in an audible way.

It confirms something we have been sensing for a while, but did not quite fully see yet. It articulates the very idea that has been slowly developing within. So when we hear this phrase it feels like a great gift of clarity. Or, it is something so true and beautiful, that we immediately believe it and desperately want to receive it for ourselves.

But…believing something and receiving something are not the same thing. Or to put it another way, believing is not the same as becoming.

So we hear spiritual teachers say these amazing phrases:

"You are unconditionally loved by God right now."

"Everything you need to be free is already within you."

"You are already enough."

And we are so excited when we hear and learn these new ideas, we can convince ourselves that we actually have fully received them and have become the truth of them immediately. We believe we haven't just learned something new, but have immediately become someone new.

Then a few days goes by, life happens, and we realize that being taught and being transformed are not exactly the same.

If everything I need to be free is within me, why do I still feel a massive sense of lack?

If I am already enough, why do I still care so much about what my co-worker Bill (who I don't even like) thinks about my new car?

If I am unconditionally loved by God, why don't I feel it and why am I not more healed and happy than I am?

There can be confusion between learning and living, or frustration with the gap that exists between information and incarnation. We feel this deep sense of struggle to overcome the divide between believing in the concept of God's love in our mind and experiencing God's love concretely for ourselves.

Usually, we are able to express to others what we have not truly experienced for ourselves. In light of all that, here is my one claim in this chapter:

When it comes to issues of awakening and experiencing God, the issue is not that you don't love God enough, it's that you won't let go enough.

Rohr claimed, "Faith at its essential core is accepting that you are accepted."

Rumi declared, "Your task is not to seek for love, but merely to seek and find all the barriers within yourself that you have built against it."

The Apostle Paul wrote, "Only let us live up to what we have already attained."

Well, there it is. I mean, how can you disagree with Richard Rohr, Rumi, and the Apostle Paul together?

What if the issue is never whether or not we are accepted, but us learning how to accept that we are accepted? What if this has nothing to do with seeking out love, and everything to do with discovering all of the barriers within that get in the way of us consciously experiencing the love that is here? What if the good news is not about attaining anything, and instead an evolutionary movement of living into what we already have?

This would radically change the spiritual journey.

Do you remember what I just said?

It's not that you don't love God enough, it's that you won't let go enough. These brilliant mystics and lovers of God are revealing one of the ultimate truths on our path of waking up and directly experiencing God for ourselves.

God is not on the way, you are in the way.

The anonymous mystic who wrote the Cloud of Unknowing in the 14th Century, speaks of a "Naked, intent, direct to God" kind of knowing of God, and being known by God.

Naked.

Exposed.

Open.

Vulnerable.

Direct.

None of that has anything to do with the One you are being known and loved by, but has everything to do with how available you are to be seen, known, and loved.

Our first apartment after we got married had a fireplace. It was the kind of fireplace that you only had to twist a knob to turn on. (Which perfectly communicates the level of woodsman I am.)

And I used to sit in front of that fire place staring at the flames in silence.

Praying.

Meditating.

Present.

And sometimes I was naked.

If you think that's weird just reading about it, imagine how weird my wife thought it was actually seeing it!

(Actually, she was even more concerned than you could imagine. I used to spend so much time in silence in front of the fireplace at night time, that sometimes she would open the door from another room and say, "Jesus. Right babe? Still Jesus?"

See, since she grew up more in the church as a teenager, she hadn't experienced someone like me who dwelled in silence, moved in the contemplative, and had this mystical kind of wiring. So, in our early twenties, between the Brian McLaren books I was reading and my extended time in silence staring at a fire, every now and then she would just double check on my salvation!)

Back to the fire place. As strange as it sounds to sit in front of a fire place naked and in prayer, for me, it was a symbolic enactment of what I would experience in contemplation.

The vulnerability of truly being seen.

The openness that allowed me to be known in unguarded intimacy.

To have nothing to hide and to still feel safe.

And to have no form of my own protection and to still be warmed by the fire (as long as I turned the knob every fifteen minutes).

This is why Nouwen said, "In solitude I get rid of my scaffolding: no friends to talk with, no telephone calls to make, no meetings to attend...just me—naked, vulnerable, weak, sinful, deprived, broken—nothing."

When we allow ourselves to become nothing, we will finally experience everything.

It is only the unguarded heart that can know real intimacy with the divine. It isn't the strength of love that decides the quality of connection in silence, it is the degree to which our entire being is open and receptive that defines the depth of union. This foundational shift is made possible through the miracle of our own naked and pure presence.

Which raises an interesting question. What's more of a miracle?

That God is present?

Or that you are?

Revelation 3:20 speaks of a God who says, "Here I am! I stand at the door and knock. If anyone hears my voice and opens the door, I will come in and eat with that person, and they with me."

The perennial mystic, Meister Eckhart says "You should know that God must act and pour Himself into you the moment He finds you ready."

The vulnerable God is waiting to be let in by the one who is daring enough to open the door of their heart. (What a different and more beautiful image than an angry God who has to punish us unless he kills his son!)

So, if it's true that when it comes to receiving love, it's never about whether we love God enough, and always about whether we let go enough, we are brought back to our re-emerging question:

What needs to be let go of in order to experience God and to receive love?

Before we get further into what it is that needs to be let go of to experience God and receive love, a quick and helpful thought. I use these two phrases—experiencing God and receiving love—virtually interchangeably, because the barriers within you that get in the way of experiencing God are the same barriers that get in the way of you receiving love.

And to receive love from anyone or anywhere is essentially to experience the substance of God, just in a less direct way. So, opening up to receive love from people, and learning how experience Spirit are inseparable companions on a mutual journey toward awakening.

Now, the first thing we need to let go of in order to experience Spirit is our attachment to false stories that prevent us from being open. These are the scripts we've unconsciously been handed in life that turn the simplicity of receiving love into a convoluted process we can never seem to untangle.

These are the kinds of hidden, unconscious, and sneaky plot lines that get in the way of the love and connection we desire. Within these stories are relentless ideas that make unguarded intimacy and openness so difficult.

"Performing for others is the only way to be accepted by others."

"Being unique and special is the only way to be recognized and desired."

"My presence will eventually become a burden."

"People only care for me because they see it as an obligation."

"No one can ever fully love unless I'm helping them and doing something for them."

Do you relate to any of these?

Though living into these stories prevents us from being vulnerable and open enough to be loved, we are addicted to them because they also keep us in control and don't allow us to be hurt.

What we need is simplicity, vulnerability, and staying open.

What we prefer is complexity, control, and remaining closed.

We think these false stories are just about our relationship with other people, but it always goes deeper. These narratives we carry within us do not only get in the way of receiving love from people, they also prevent us from experiencing the presence of God.

Being open to anything makes you more open to everything.

Being closed to anything makes you more closed to everything.

Which is why the great Italian mystic, St. Catherine of Genoa said, "Just as a covered object left out in the sun cannot be penetrated by the sun's rays, in the same way, once the covering of the soul is removed, the soul opens itself fully to the rays of the sun. The more the rust of sin is consumed by fire, the more the soul responds to that love, and its joy increases."

And the love the soul responds to is both directly from God, or mediated through other people.

In the fall of 2016, Christine and I were at an event in Washington D.C. My wife was seven months pregnant and helping host the event, we were both presenting at the event, and it was hotter in D.C. than I knew it could even get.

(Normally whenever I travel anywhere from Hawaii, I want to go somewhere cold. And by cold I mean 65 degrees.)

So we were in D.C. for this great event at a historic location, we got to see old friends and co-laborers, and it was wonderful.

On the final night, we were in a time of worship and communion, and the great leader and writer Deb Hirsch came over to my wife and I, gave us some encouraging words and asked if she could pray for us and for our baby.

A leader and woman whom we both adore and admire wants to bless us and our child.

Sounds simple and good right?

But it wasn't.

While she was affirming and encouraging us, and as she started to tell us she wanted to pray for us, I could feel my ego begin to contract and my heart start to close off because one of my old stories was arising.

"She has to say this. She doesn't truly mean this. She says stuff like this to everyone. Whatever, I'll just sit here and go through the motions while she does it."

See, I've always had this weird suspicion of people in authority. I've always questioned their motives, and have always initially doubted their care for me. This inherited narrative made a part of me believe that someone in authority who I respect and admire could never be genuinely interested in me, or enjoy my presence.

This story always made me feel like a burden to people I admire. Like somehow I'm going to stick around too long, wear out my welcome, and become an obligatory presence that they're secretly hoping to get away from.

So in that moment, I could hear the voice of this old story telling me not to trust her or allow her words in. That it would make me look like a fool for believing her and accepting her love for us because she didn't really mean it.

And I could feel this old story trying to keep me closed off, make me shut down, and force me to go through the motions without truly allowing myself to open up. If this story remained in place, it would not allow me to take in the connection of the moment, and to receive the goodness that was flowing to me.

Do you see how these narratives we carry within us not only get in the way of receiving love from people, but also prevent us from experiencing the presence of God? Can you feel in that story how love, grace, connection, and

Spirit were all present, and it was my own distorted story that was getting in the way of me receiving everything I desired?

So what happened?

I recognized the protective story for the lie that it was, dis-identified with it, allowed it to pass by me, surrendered, and fell into the love of the moment. And yes, love is always something we truly fall into.

And then of course, I cried.

When I released, relaxed, and let go of this old misguided narrative, I could feel my ego completely uncoil, the horizon of my being expand, and my heart open up freely enough to receive the love that was flowing and the Spirit that was pouring out.

Then I cried some more.

There are stories we all need to let go of to be more open to love.

There are stories at work in you that are getting in the way of God.

There are plot lines in your mind that you've used to protect yourself from being hurt, that are now preventing you from being loved.

There are old scripts that keep trying to get you to read the same lines and stay the same character, but there is a new story you are called into, and it is one that always concludes with you being loved.

In more mature stages of faith, the defining tension for growth, experience, and being known by God is never whether you have been good or bad, it is always whether you are open or closed.

Spirit is infinitely pouring itself out through this universe.

Love, in its self-giving nature, is always giving itself to you.

Grace just is.

So, are we opened up or shut down? Available or distracted? Allowing or rejecting?

The stories we have trusted that have helped us in our survival dance in the first half of life, need to be laid down in order to move into our sacred dance through the second half of life.

Without even knowing it, we all walk around with so many parts of us closed off and in a defensive posture. Which means there are spaces within that are unknowable by the presence of God, and unreachable by grace. This is why the next thing we have to let go of in order to be open to God are all of the different kinds of protection we have around our heart.

Did you know that the same armor that protects your heart from being hurt also prevents your heart from knowing God, receiving love, and experiencing grace?

One of the many invaluable concepts popularized and normalized by the work of Brené Brown is the idea of *foreboding joy*.

Foreboding joy is essentially when we close our self off from experiencing the fullness of joy because we are worried about the object of joy being taken from us. Brown writes, "When something good happens, our immediate thought is that we'd better not let ourselves truly feel it, because if we really love something we could lose it."

And so, instead of accepting the possibility of pain that comes from losing what we have, we forebode our joy and never fully allow ourselves to receive it in the first place.

Brown brilliantly says that in each of these moments, we are

"dress rehearsing tragedy," and "trying to beat disappointment to the punch."

We close ourselves off from the possibility of loss, which means we shut our hearts down from the fullness of joy.

The profound truth of Brown's clarifying claim of foreboding joy, extends beyond the experience of joy, and applies to the experience of everything good.

Without even realizing it, we can also be

foreboding love,

foreboding grace,

end even foreboding Spirit.

In Mark 8:31-33, Jesus has this defining interaction with Peter. Jesus is talking about how suffering, rejection, and death are essential parts of his path, which really means they are all essential parts of the path of being fully human. But when Peter hears this, he recoils, resists, and reacts aggressively toward Jesus.

"He then began to teach them that the Son of Man must suffer many things and be rejected by the elders, the chief priests and the teachers of the law, and that he must be killed and after three days rise again. He spoke plainly about this, and Peter took him aside and began to rebuke him. But when Jesus turned and looked at his disciples, he rebuked Peter. "Get behind me, Satan!" he said. "You do not have in mind the concerns of God, but merely human concerns."

What makes Peter's rebuke even more interesting, was right before this interaction, Peter had just declared that Jesus was indeed the Messiah. And now when Jesus starts to talk about the suffering he will experience and the rejection he is going to face, Peter rebukes Jesus. Peter is challenging Jesus because he is unwilling to include the suffering and death that Jesus had already accepted.

He loves the way, the truth, and the life, but he's resisting the pain, the struggle, and the death.

For Peter, the darkness is unthinkable, but for Jesus, it is inevitable.

Since Peter could not accept the cross, he could not embrace the Christ.

I still do that sometimes.

We fear, reject, and cannot accept how painful things might be, and as a result are unable to trust and know how present God is. Since we cannot accept how hard that might be, we cannot experience how good this is. We cannot include that, so we never fully receive this.

Because there is this, and there is also that.

There's this.

The place where I hear the One Voice telling me who I am, while other voices try to convince me of who I'm not. The place where I receive, as a free gift, the love I am tempted to try to earn from others. The place where I wake up to what is real, and see with clarity what is fake. The place where I experience the connection, intimacy, and fidelity of God in a world where relationships are broken and nothing is guaranteed. The place where I dare to go into the depth of my own darkness, only to discover that all that's at the bottom is light. The place where I touch the ground of all being, and feel that it's only made of grace.

And there's that.

The possibility that if I resist the part of me that wants to hold back and protect myself, and choose to try my hardest, I still might fail. The possibility that if I take the risk of beginning again, I could end up dealing with the same criticism and rejection that made me want to shut down in the first place. The possibility that the people I love might leave. The terror that the creative offering I pour out might spill onto the floor of life with the uninspiring thud of indifference.

We all want This.

But we can't accept that.

But, unless we learn the art of embracing and including that, we will always miss out on This.

***

Recently, I pulled up to a stop sign and I was singing Miley Cyrus' song "Wrecking Ball" at the top of my lungs. I virtually memorized the lyrics to Katy Perry's song, "Roar," I keep whispering the phrase, "I am Superwoman" from Alicia Keys, and have had Rihanna's hit, "Diamonds," on repeat.

First, I love all these songs.

Second, Let me explain.

My four year old daughter Mikayla Brave and I recently made a special playlist together on Spotify. Every song is either an upbeat, feel good song, or some kind of inspiration jam or ballad about overcoming, sung by a woman. This is one of the many fun ways I can help my little girl become a strong and independent woman.

(Did you catch that?)

So my daughter, my two year old son, and I were pulling into the beach park we always go to. And while we were looking for parking, we were all singing Beyonce's beautiful song, "Halo." I'm singing at a volume that is too low to be heard, but still flowing from an unusually deep place within. My son is contributing by basically making the vowel sound of every last word of each line. And my daughter is singing the chorus with her whole heart and cute little squeaky voice.

And the way she kept repeating the word halo from the chorus was just completely undoing me. It was like I was being utterly taken apart and put back together by each sound that came out of her mouth.

I was in love.

Like, actually in love.

In my car, sitting in the ever present flow of love.

And then I thought about her growing up.

In this unexpected flash of the future, I could see the inevitable loss of innocence that eventually gets the best of all of us. I could foresee the inescapable pain she would go through during distinct and defining moments of her adolescence.

I knew it would not always be this simple.

And I immediately felt the helplessness and vulnerability of knowing that there was no way I could protect her from this. I could feel the horror of allowing our hearts to be so dangerously open in this world, and in that moment, felt the exact reason why its so easy to close ourselves off from the sacred when we are face to face with the possibility of loss.

I could have held back. I could have shut down a little bit. I could have been so worried about the potential loss in the future, that it could have robbed me of the love in the present.

But I didn't.

I just let it all in.

I refused to shut any part of me down out of the fear of suffering and hurt.

I would not miss the miracle of my kids because I was scared.

I soaked in the magic of my four year old's innocent voice and gulped down the reality of the struggle we will all face.

I allowed myself to be in the fullness of love flowing through Beyonce's voice in the sanctuary of our messy Toyota Rav-4. And this sacred experience was only possible through accepting the inability to control my children's life and protect them from the Good Fridays I know they are going to have.

In that sacred and scary moment, my only task was to keep my heart open and allow love to be.

My decision to let go of the need to exclude pain from our lives, and to surrender and entrust my beautiful and vulnerable children to the presence of God, is what allowed love to flow so freely in that space. Letting go of the impossible need to always protect my children, enabled me to enjoy my children, and experience God.

So remember.

It's never about whether we love God enough, it's always about whether we let go enough.

Five

GROWING AND EVOLVING

During a break from our event, a group of us were eating an early dinner and having a drink before we all returned for the night session. We were all in New York City for a gathering that brought together some of the leading thinkers on contemplative spirituality, the unfolding nature of consciousness, and what the faith of the future might look like.

My Bible College professors would not approve.

As we were eating, I went off on an unfiltered and epic rant. Which I will admit, is normal dinner time conversation for me.

Although I do not remember the exact nature of the playful tirade, I am sure I was talking about the difference between waking up and growing up, the limitations of beliefs to actually transform us, how direct experience of Spirit is the grounding substance of everything, and how the mystic is the one who takes life so seriously that they don't have to take it seriously at all.

You know? Normal stuff.

As I was finishing, one of the guys at the table was just smirking.

This is a guy from the south who is much more at home in the conservative Christian household than I am, and who seems comfortable living within the current conditions of evangelicalism. And also, just a genuinely nice guy.

When I finished, he told me that listening to me talk is like getting on a bus and going for a grand adventure. And while on this exciting journey, he said everything he sees out the window is so beautiful, seems so exciting, and looks like this unparalleled atmosphere of freedom.

Yet he finished this description by saying, "But I just can't go there with you."

Very interesting.

He sees beauty, excitement, and freedom.

But he can't go with me.

Which of course raises the question. Why? Why would someone get a glimpse of an increased experience of freedom and beauty and still decide to stay where they are?

Are they scared?

If so,

What are they scared of?

That they won't fit back in their church? That they'll lose their job in ministry? That they've gone too far from home? Scared that if they open up to new ways of seeing God, they aren't sure where they're going to end up on the spectrum of belief? Maybe they're worried that God might be mad at them? Or punish them? Or that somehow a free movement forward might create a threat to their financial well being?

This story reveals the complicated relationship we have with growth.

There's nothing we want more than real transformation and nothing we resist more than change. We dream of a future that is more liberated and empowered, and yet consistently avoid the spaces that can lead us to this future. We long to be surprised with a genuine experience of newness from

God, but we keep holding on to the false sense of comfort from the old personal and cosmic grooves we are in.

Too often, we choose what is familiar over what is freeing.

But here's the thing.

Change is never about betraying where you've been, it's always about becoming who you are.

Jesus never critiqued people for widening the circle of inclusion, only those who were making it smaller.

Jesus never got angry with people whose view of God and life was expanding, only with those that refused to grow.

Not once did Jesus scold someone who was creating the Spirit's future, but he did challenge everyone who kept re-creating their tradition's past.

He directly said to some of the Pharisees, "You have let go of the commands of God and are holding on to human traditions." And he continued, "You have a fine way of setting aside the commands of God in order to observe your own traditions!"

They were holding onto traditions that were getting in the way of the outward expanding movement of the Spirit. The religious leaders' attempt to hold onto God was now getting in the way of the movement of God.

Ken Wilber writes, "God lies down the road, not up it; Spirit is found by going forward, not backward; the Garden of Eden lies in our future, not our past."

The path keeps getting wider.

God becomes even more embracing.

And you feel more and more like you.

No matter how scary it feels each time you approach the edge of the boundaries of your self and gaze beyond the mysterious threshold of growth, the movement of the Spirit is always carried forward by those who are courageous enough to keep stepping beyond.

So, let's think about change.

One of the great pioneers of the Christian tradition, the apostle Paul, became the icon that he is because he changed.

He wrote in Galatians 1:13-16

"For you have heard of my previous way of life in Judaism, how intensely I persecuted the church of God and tried to destroy it. I was advancing in Judaism beyond many of my own age among my people and was extremely zealous for the traditions of my fathers. But when God, who set me apart from my mother's womb and called me by his grace, was pleased **to reveal** *his Son in me so that I might preach him among the Gentiles, my immediate response was not to consult any human being."*

Paul believed in God passionately, and then God revealed Himself more.

The Spirit disclosed more of the mystery, and when these lights turned on, Paul could see with more clarity. And when this revealing took place, his view of God and humanity was radically changed.

Paul went from a narrow and exclusive view of God that came from his tradition, to a wider and more inclusive view that was revealed in Jesus.

This was a revolutionary shift.

To put it in perspective.

It would be like Sean Hannity acknowledging the need for Critical Race Theory.

Or Laura Ingram leading a march for Black Lives Matter.

Or Donald Trump saying, "I was wrong. I'm sorry."

Now, do you see how shocking this change would have been for Paul?

Paul was the most committed, devout, and faithful believer you could imagine. He was completely certain of what he believed, but when God revealed Himself to him in an unexpected way, he realized he was partially wrong, that his view of God was limited and that he needed to grow in his understanding of the mystery.

Besides Jesus, the most influential voice in the early history of our faith became who he was and did what he did because he allowed his view of God, humanity, and himself to change.

Like I said, the path keeps getting wider.

And yet, even though it is the voice of Christ who spoke to Paul, and one of the greatest leaders in our tradition who changed so radically, our household of faith still seems so resistant to change and is still so scared of growth.

What do we lose when we change that is so traumatic to release? Why can it be scary to grow? Why do we hold onto beliefs about God that keep getting in the way of our future?

Which is why the next question is obvious, what do we need to let go of in order to grow and change?

I was twenty four years old, sitting in the back of a church in Hawaii, and listening to one of the most ridiculous and dangerous sermons I've ever heard. This well respected and popular preacher was talking about the military and war, how the devil and demons attack us, and other ideas I'm sure a part of me blocked out immediately after I heard them.

It was magical and mythical thinking, fear mongering nationalism, and somehow this man still had the audacity to conclude with an altar call.

After all of that?

An altar call?

Really?

What exactly were people supposed to say yes to?

Despite my disbelief that someone could preach this sermon and be confident enough to end with an altar call, I still unexpectedly responded to that moment in tears. Just not for the reasons other people in that auditorium would have probably assumed. While people around me thought this gifted preacher just led another troubled young man into the presence of the Lord, the truth was,

I wept because I knew I could never be a part of churches like this.

I wept because I knew there were so many relationships I wouldn't have because of the trajectory of my growth.

I wept because I felt the immediacy of uncertainty, loneliness, and loss of connection that would continue to be associated with my unfolding journey in Christ.

Which is why the first thing we need to let go of in order to grow is some of our relationships.

Now, this does not mean that as you evolve, you need to walk away from people who are not going where you're going. It simply means we need to accept that some people will walk away from us as we grow. The same people who were once supportive and encouraging of who we were are now worried and concerned about where we're going. While they might see faith as a straight path you are supposed to stay committed to, you see it as an ever widening road that keeps getting more expansive and inclusive.

They're certain you're crossing over the lines, you're confident the road keeps widening.

It might also mean that the people you cherished as guides and mentors before can no longer fulfill that role for you on new stages of your journey. To listen to the same people who used to help you grow can now feel like an unwelcome beckoning that is drawing you backwards.

That's okay.

The transformation of your teachers and guides into guardians of a past you want nothing to do with is painful, can be frustrating, and is sometimes confusing. To lose these people we deeply cherished is a form of relational death we will have to learn how to grieve and accept along the way. But as we learn to accept this, we will discover that we can still love and appreciate them, even while we no longer look to them to guide us anymore.

Sometimes, in totally unexpected ways, our spiritual growth and development is going to even change our friendships.

This one can really suck.

Religious people who believe their primary task is to get others to believe what they believe or see how they see, will see it as impossible to simply remain friends while you are changing into a shape that does not fit into their religious container. Since they (unconsciously) see their acceptance of you as a kind of condoning of where you are going—which is a place they not only see as problematic, but are convinced God does too—to be a friend is to be an accomplice to your destruction.

What kind of a friend would they be to just sit back and watch as you "lose" your faith?

To include you in their life would be to condone where you're going, and they feel they have an obligation to God to ensure that you do not keep going forward on your current path.

I know this one might sound weird.

But many of us know how real it is to lose friendships and have people we love slowly create distance because our current stage of spirituality does not fit into their understanding of faith.

Other times it means that we can no longer be a part of the institutions, communities, or churches we once called home. One of the reasons why reflecting on our relationships with communities is so urgent while we are growing is this:

The need for institutional acceptance is a massive wall that gets in the way of individual growth.

Have you ever had one of those sacred moments where we get a glimpse of a different future?

We read something that becomes a spotlight that enables us to see ahead in ways our community seems unable to. We have an experience that lifts us above our current framework, enlightens our eyes to see the limitations of our current system, and thus liberates our vision to see beyond it. We develop a friendship with someone whose very presence leaves us unhinged, and ready to enlarge our entire sense of Self.

And when this happens, our ego can immediately see all of the ways this puts us at odds with our community and could leave us unsettled in our beloved institutions. And because these glimpses are experienced as threats to our social self, we are tempted to want to cover our eyes from these rays of light from the Spirit that have come to blaze a new trail.

I know. It can be scary to grow.

But eventually, integrity means we cannot lead the same way we used to. Authenticity requires us to challenge the way things are, which also means the institution we once loved might not be a part of us committing to create the way things can be. The people who once saw you as a gift in the community might now see you as a threat to the community.

Which is a horrible feeling.

If a group of us were together, we could go on about all of the unique expressions of relational losses we've experienced due to our growth and the nature of how we've changed. The awkward and strangely tense conversations with old friends. The weird and hurtful comments we hear others who we've known and respected say about who we are or where we're going. The deep concern we discern others feel for us when, to be honest, we're actually doing better than ever. The way groups of people who were once a part of our life seem to pull away at a pace that is not felt immediately, but is undeniable over a longer period of time.

Guess what?

That's okay.

It's all okay.

It's all a normal part of a life that refuses to ever settle, crust over, and remain the same.

One of the key dynamics we need to let go of on our unique journey of transformation is the need for any relationships to stay exactly the same as we grow. Dogmatic religious people are some of the most fearful people you will know, and when they feel threatened by your movement forward, you will find out.

Your growth is going to offend people.

Your freedom is going to scare people.

Your change is going to challenge people.

Not everyone is going to go where you're going, see what you've seen, or become who you're becoming. And the deep ego need for people to approve of us, agree with us, or even understand us at any point on our path is going to become one of the biggest obstacles on the pathway to the future the Spirit is calling us into.

In Mark 7:6-9, Jesus is challenging the religious leaders' view of God, and their understanding of how to live faithfully before God.

He replied, "Isaiah was right when he prophesied about you hypocrites; as it is written:

"'These people honor me with their lips,

but their hearts are far from me.

They worship me in vain;

their teachings are merely human rules.'

You have let go of the commands of God and are holding on to human traditions."

And he continued, "You have a fine way of setting aside the commands of God in order to observe your own traditions!

This story shows how Jesus comes along and keeps challenging, subverting, and calling people beyond their current understanding of God. He is not telling people not to believe in God, he is showing people an image of God that is fuller, more beautiful, and even more faithful to their sacred scriptures. By challenging their view of God, he's not calling people away from God, he's actually calling them closer to God.

Jesus was seen as a threat not because he didn't believe in God, but because he didn't believe in their version of God.

And this can happen to us too.

We can live with this radical permission to allow change to be the constant state we are in as we are consistently formed and re-formed by the Spirit, we just need to be willing to let go of any relationships that are trying to disrupt this flow. You are going to be misunderstood, you are going to be misrepresented, it's really hard when it happens, and it's probably going to hurt. But we can trust and know that all of that hurt is the temporary cost for more freedom, more joy, and a deeper life with God.

Growth is always worth it.

The second thing we need to let go of in order to grow is security.

Now, before we move forward, I want to be absolutely clear. When I say that in order to grow we need to let go of our security, I do not mean that as we keep evolving we become less and less secure, it's actually quite the opposite. As we grow up and wake up more and more, we naturally become more grounded, more secure, and organically live more from the deepest center in Christ.

So, when I say we need to let go of security to change, what that means is the relinquishing of any false sense of security that helped hold us together in the previous stages of our life.

We have to let go of what we thought was our security in order to feel secure.

We have to let go of what used to make us feel at home, in order to truly feel at home in ourselves.

We have to let go of what we use to hold onto, so we can experience the freedom of not needing to hold onto anything.

Ken Wilber writes, "Transformative spirituality, authentic spirituality, is therefore revolutionary. It does not legitimate the world, it breaks the world; it does not console the world, it shatters it. And it does not render the self content, it renders it undone."

Are you encouraged yet?

No?

Okay, then let's take it even further.

Every time you take a giant evolutionary step, each moment you cross over a threshold into a new stage, and any instance where you dare to transcend the previous boundaries of your self,

you die.

We can't really take it further than that can we?

But it's true. Every time you grow, a part of you dies.

You die to that old self. You die to your old forms of security. You die to that old sense of familiarity. You die to things that used to bring you comfort. You die to the entire internal structure and system that used to create the needed experience of security in that stage of your life.

Wilber also says, "...each time the self identifies with a particular level of consciousness it experiences the loss of that level as a death—literally, as a type of death-seizure, because the very life of the self is identified with that level."

So, whenever you are going to change, you have to prepare to die.

I remember sitting in the back one of my first classes in grad school, and I started to feel a little weird. My body got flush, I became slightly light headed, and I even felt a little woozy.

A disconnect between my mind and body started emerging, and for some reason when this was happening, my mind started racing, and I started to think about where I was with my beliefs and what I was currently reading on my journey.

"Why am I reading Jean Luc Marion's *God Without Being*?" "Where am I even going in my faith?" "What do I even believe anymore?" "Where is this all going to take me?"

As these questions were rapidly firing off in my mind, and my body was still feeling strange and unaligned, I stepped out of the class to gather myself. I bought some sour gummy bears, got something to drink, sat down, and after I started eating the candy, I started to feel normal. After my mind and body settled, I returned to class, kept reading my same books, and was more confident than ever about where I was going.

Turned out it wasn't a crisis of faith, it was just low blood sugar!

But that story speaks to how temporarily disruptive and distressing going through radical personal change and spiritual growth can feel.

Unsettling.

Disruptive.

Stripping down.

Dismantling.

Foundation shifting.

Anxiety provoking.

But the unfolding path of spiritual growth communicates to us again and again that what feels like a loss in the foundation of your faith is actually the Spirit inviting you to the future of your faith.

This is why Wilber writes, "...remember that belief systems are not merely beliefs—they are the home of the ego, the home of the self-contraction."

Your beliefs are not just some casual parts of who you are. What Wilber rightfully claims is that your beliefs are the very house your ego takes up residence in and dwells in for its entire sense of safety. Your separate self needs these beliefs because it believes it *is* these beliefs. To lose your beliefs is to lose what you think is your self. Which is exactly why when someone challenges your beliefs, it feels like they are threatening your home.

This is why growing is so scary.

This is why we treat change like death.

This is why defending our beliefs can feel like we're fighting for our life.

But to surrender beliefs that are no longer serving us is like moving out of the house that we used to build our life, only to discover there is a much bigger dwelling space waiting for us. Perhaps this is why the great mystic Hafiz said, "Fear is the cheapest room in the house. I'd like to see you in better living conditions."

When it comes to beliefs, too many people treat temporary settlements as their permanent housing.

The beliefs we thought once saved us will eventually no longer serve us.

The ideas that used to help us will one day can become a hindrance to us.

The map of reality that was leading us five years ago has become outdated and no longer has the capacity to lead you ahead.

So do we lose a sense of security when we let go and grow?

Yes.

But we also discover that the security we lost was something we never needed to feel safe in the first place.

I never really believed in the rapture.

The idea that at the end of the world, there are going to be catastrophes, violence, wars, and that the people who had faith in Jesus would be beamed up to heaven through some neon blue (not sure why I assume it would be blue) portal as a means of escaping all the suffering, just seemed ridiculous to me.

The notion that the good news of this universe looked like some weird religious sci-fi movie that somehow had The United States of America at the center of it seemed a bit odd and dangerously ethnocentric, even for the United States.

But a lot of people do believe this.

And while I was attending a Christian college, this was the dominant view in the school.

Which is why one afternoon when I was about twenty three years old, and reading by our apartment pool, I started to get sick to my stomach. I was reading a book called, "A Christianity Worth Believing,"

(Which is an amazing title because it carries within it the assumption that there are versions of Christianity that are not worth believing.)

and the future vision of new creation, a healed world, and the beautiful idea of heaven and earth becoming one just clicked. The good news of a God not abandoning the planet during a time of suffering and turmoil, but a God who wipes every tear, ends every injustice, heals all of creation, and re-creates the world as a whole hit me with the weight of all of its beauty and power.

And right as it happened, my heart sunk, my stomach started to hurt, and a shock wave of anxiety rippled through my body.

Why would the most beautiful vision of the universe be followed by a moment of personal fright?

I immediately knew that because of my beliefs, my relationships at the school would change. I immediately felt the possibility of being on the fringes of the institution, the edges of the community, and the oncoming relational antagonism.

I also felt strangely alone and vulnerable. Although I never truly bought into the idea of the rapture or the "end times" (as its commonly understood), making this internal shift to fully disagree with it created this immediate sense of fragility. To move from indifference to an old idea to conviction for the new one made me highly aware of my own contingency and agency in life.

And do you know what happened after this defining moment of seeing the beauty of the future and experiencing the loss in the present?

Nothing.

And by nothing, I mean nothing horrible happened.

Sure, one of my professors challenged me to debate him or "take him on" on this issue, while I was unprepared and still developing my understanding on it.

And yeah, at a friend's birthday party, someone told me they couldn't believe that on judgment day, I was going to stand before Jesus and tell him I didn't believe in the rapture. (Which by the way, is hilarious.)

And of course, one time I did get approached by a pastor at my old church seeking clarification because I wrote on my facebook status, "The rapture is a myth."

Yes, it changed my relationship with some institutions, meant I could not fit or pastor in some of the religious spaces my friends could be a part of, and created some distance or weirdness with people or communities,

but none of that mattered.

My vision for the planet was hopeful, my understanding of our sacred task to partner with the Spirit to work for healing was empowering, and my freedom to create the future was liberating my imagination in a way that old vision could never do.

Whenever we are fearful of growing, we have to remember that the only things we lose are our chains, and all we ever let go of are the things getting in the way of our freedom.

It is always the Spirit calling us forward.

Always.

This is why I love when Mirabai Starr writes, "...so there is rejoicing in heaven when God removes the baby clothes from the soul. He is setting her down from his arms and making her walk on her own two feet."

So celebrate every time you rip another piece of those baby clothes off of your soul, and walk freely into the future with the Spirit that is always inviting you further.

Six

PEACE

There is this provocative ancient Hindu story about being cold, a falcon, and an unexpected visit to hell.

One day Lal Shabaz Qalander was wandering in the desert with his friend Sheikh Baha ud-Din Zakariya. It was freezing and as the evening came they decided to build a fire to keep warm while they camped. They gathered some wood and built a pyre, but then realized that they had no way to ignite it. So Baha ud-Din suggested that Lal Shabaz turn himself into a falcon, fly down and bring some fire from hell.

Off he flew, and hours passed. Eventually the bird-god soared back to Baha ud-Din, and fluttered to his side, empty-handed. Cold and bewildered Baha ud-Din asked him why he had not brought fire back with him. "There is no fire in hell," he reported, changing back into his usual form. "Everyone who goes there from this world brings their own."

Interesting.

There is no fire in hell.

Or, to put it more accurately, the only fire in hell is the kind we bring ourselves.

Now, before people get all 2010, when everybody was scared and angry at Rob Bell for writing "Love Wins," let's assume that this parable is not about a literal place called hell that we might either go to or not go to when we die. Instead, assume that this story has something profound to say about what it means to experience peace while we live.

Some of the first words I remember reading from Jesus after my initial encounter with God were these light, playful, and provocative thoughts about birds. He mentioned the freedom of birds and flowers, a life lived without worry, and how if we seek God first, everything else will organically fall into place.

Birds. Flowers. And living without worry.

Trust me.

He actually said these things.

I know it sounds like your roommate from your Sophomore year of college right after they hit the blunt. But I'm serious, it was Jesus.

In Matthew 6, he said,

"Therefore I tell you, do not worry about your life, what you will eat or drink; or about your body, what you will wear. Is not life more than food, and the body more than clothes?"

"Look at the birds of the air; they do not sow or reap or store away in barns, and yet your heavenly Father feeds them. Are you not much more valuable than they?"

"See how the flowers of the field grow...

"But seek first his kingdom and his righteousness, and all these things will be given to you as well. Therefore do not worry about tomorrow, for tomorrow will worry about itself. Each day has enough trouble of its own."

Told you.

All Jesus.

What struck my twenty year old mind and heart as I read these playful, yet revolutionary words, was the vision from Jesus that we can actually be at peace. That we can be free. I also believed there was a way of being and an approach to life that allows us to live without worry. And Jesus spoke the possibility of that path into existence for me.

When I was seventeen years old, I remember sitting outside of my plug's house (If you know what a plug is, you know what I'm saying. If you don't know what a plug is, don't even worry about it.) and thinking to my self,

"I just want to be…"

And as silly as that might sound, within that seventeen year old groaning was the depth of frustration from that universal feeling like there is always something more we need to achieve in order to be at peace. And the desire to break free from that cycle of doing more and more to attain something that never comes.

Don't we all want that?

To be able to just be?

And be at peace.

Three years later, reading those words of Jesus was like breathing fresh air for the first time, because he knew. He knew it was possible to be at peace. He knew there was a way to transcend worry. And no matter how naïve many people believe that is, he was daring to articulate a way of being that had peace integrated into it's day to day flow.

For Jesus, peace is possible.

Which brings us back to the parable about hell in the beginning.

In Matthew 6, Jesus shows us that we can be at peace.

The parable reveals that the only things getting in the way of peace exist within us. Or, to say it another way, the only flames that exist in hell are the ones we bring ourselves.

So, there is the possibility of peace, and there are the myriad things that are stuck to us and seem to refuse to let us go—things that keep ruining the possibility of peace.

Let me pose some questions that can begin to help us see that it is things within that get in the way of peace.

What is going to bring us peace?

Acquiring more or requiring less?

Getting the moment to go exactly like we wanted or surrendering the moment to the Spirit?

Having all of our expectations met or letting go of our expectations?

Fighting to win an argument or transcending the need to win?

These questions are merely a glimpse into the way in which our way of being in the world carry the potential to either block the path of peace, or clear the way for peace. Every single one of these questions is not about whether or not the peace Jesus talked about is possible, they are about whether or not we are going to get in the way of the peace we all long for.

You are more powerful than you realize when it comes to this journey toward peace. Jesus gave us the vision of this radical sense of peace, but you have the power to live into that vision and become that person of peace in ways you don't even know.

We have been created for peace.

Which raises our refrain of a question: What do we need to let go of in order to be at peace?

The first thing we need to let go of in order to experience peace is the need for approval.

We spend an exorbitant amount of energy trying to "save face." So let's begin with this question: What do we mean when we say we are attempting to save face?

Well, it means we are doing what we can to avoid embarrassment and humiliation, or to escape the ever present fear of being exposed. At an internal light speed, we strategically maneuver, leverage power, practice timely name drops, avoid sharing specific details of stories, exaggerate events that have happened, deny truths within, try to impress others, or omit parts of our story—all for the sake of saving face.

And ninety-nine percent of the time, we are not even aware we are doing this.

This ongoing practice of saving face raises even more intriguing questions:

Whose face are we trying to save? Who exactly are we afraid is going to be exposed? Or, what if being exposed is actually an open door and invitation to more wholeness?

The ego is constantly hustling to save face, and peace is the discovery that this face we keep trying to save isn't truly ours.

The face we try to save is simply the face of the false self and ego that is the barrier to peace in the first place.

Let me give you a brief glimpse into my life, and the life of pastors and preachers. When you preach for years and give hundreds or thousands of sermons, you have all kinds of interesting things happen.

A couple sits way too close to the front with their dog and make it hard to move around.

People defiantly walk out during the sermon as a way of putting their distaste of your teaching on display.

You give everything you have to preach this revolutionary message that can radically upend people's entire lives, and someone sleeps through it.

You interact with the crowd during a sermon only to be publicly disrupted and challenged by The Flash from The Justice League movie (that's a long story).

But by far, my most unique experience preaching happened in 2017, when I was asked to help lead a house church for the six week winter surf season on the North Shore of Oahu. For those who don't know, every year from the beginning of November to the middle of December, the global surf community descends onto the North Shore for Triple Crown Season.

This is like the Super Bowl of surfing.

Professional surfers, media outlets, corporate brands, up and coming hopefuls, and people just looking to be a part of the party all gather in this one place for one of the most unique athletic seasons in professional sports.

So during this season in 2017, a friend of mine asked me to help her lead this house church, and preach each Thursday night for six weeks.

Seems simple enough.

But this was a house filled with professional surfers, notorious North Shore figures who are universally feared, young emerging surfers from Tahiti who barely spoke English, and enough ego and pride to make smiling during my teaching seem like it was against the law.

Everyone there existed somewhere on the scale from I know exactly why I'm here, to I'm not even sure what is happening right now.

I'm going to be honest.

It was a tough crowd.

Each night as I was drawing from the depths of my creative being in order to give the best stuff I had, I finally knew what it felt like to be a stand up comedian who was bombing and still had to finish their set.

I'm not saying that it wasn't good, but I'm definitely saying that it was hard.

And at times, I'm surprised my wife didn't spontaneously combust from the second hand anxiety that was exploding in her body while watching me preach to this unresponsive crowd.

On one of the nights, I was talking about how, as human beings we are thirsty for more. How it looks like a million different things—peace, joy, happiness, salvation, connection, validation—and how this foundational thirst is driving us at all times. I went on to start naming all of the ways we attempt to quench this thirst for peace outside of ourselves. I go on to say something like,

You don't have to keep trying to prove yourself.

You don't need those people's approval.

You don't need those people to recognize you.

Nothing brand new or shocking. I was simply showing how we keep asking other people to give to us what only the Spirit can give. How it is dangerous and fragile to look to others to be seen, or for validation, because the moment the applause ends, so does our experience of our sense of self.

At the end of the night, one of the international surfers who I assumed tuned me out and wrote me off during the teaching came up to me and asked if we could meet up during one of the next couple of days to talk.

So a couple of days later, we sat down on one of the most famous stretches of beach in the world, and we discussed everything I talked about the previous night.

While we were going to unexpected depths in this young man's life, another very intense and well known pro surfer from a different country comes up to us and sits with us for a bit. After being filled in on the topic of discussion, he proceeds to go off on this long and articulate description about how he lives for the high that comes from the applause of people. He talks about the intensity of competition, and the pinnacle moment of winning a Championship Tour contest and being carried up the beach by friends while the entire crowd cheers for him.

He finishes by saying, "That's what I live for. That's the high I'm always chasing."

Immediately after this outspoken and intense surfer finished his rant and said bye to both of us, the guy I was sitting with asked, "Didn't he just say he does the exact thing that you said is the problem?

With no hesitation, I whispered back, "Yes, but I sure as hell ain't gonna be the one who tells him that!"

Here's the point.

The one thing that defined his life is the very thing he will eventually need to let go of in order to be at peace. What he did not realize he was saying to us was that his entire pursuit in life is the applause from other people,

which is really getting approval from other people,

which is basically about being validated by other people,

which is ultimately about receiving our value from other people.

We can never be at peace when the ground we walk on is made up of other people's opinions about us. Our shaky sense of self will always be anxious when we live and die with every uncontrollable interaction with others. When we have unknowingly given other people the power to control our peace, we will never know the peace that only the Spirit gives.

If I need any form of approval from any human being in order to be at peace, I will not truly become peace. There will always be a part of me performing for peace, which means there will always be a part of me that does not know peace.

As we more deeply let go of the need for approval, we move away from pretending, hustling for approval, and morphing for others, and begin to move toward honesty, simplicity, and authenticity.

This is the move that leads us to freedom.

This is what leads us to peace. This is what leads us to the knowing that we are seen by eyes of God at all times. This is what enables us to know in the depths of our being that we already are what we seek.

Which is probably why Rumi said, "You wander from room to room hunting for the diamond necklace that is already around your neck."

At the center of the universe is a set of eyes who looks upon us with a gaze of shocking approval and unconditional love.

It is in this ever present and affirmative gaze, we discover that in peace, there is no performing.

The second thing we need to let go of in order to experience peace is particularity.

Here's what I mean.

The less particular you need things to be to experience peace, the more you will experience peace. And the more particular you need things to be to experience peace, the less you will experience peace.

Do you see how simple that is?

Our attachment to a specific structure of the moment is what constantly limits our capacity to experience peace in the moment.

In our day to day experience, particularity is about expectations and always carrying around some version of the way we think things are supposed to go. Particularity is an attachment to a specific form of circumstances or an ideal shape of each instance of reality. It is us unconsciously forming a version of what is supposed to happen, and then getting stuck to it or fixated on it.

Because of course, eventually what happens? Things do not go the way you envisioned them going.

The beautiful scenic picnic with your kids is chaotic and stressful. (Is it ever not?)

Your mom doesn't respond to the good news you were sharing the way you thought she would. (Has she ever?!)

The fight you're having in your relationship doesn't fit into what you thought a marriage was supposed to be. (What does that even mean?)

Your family gets into a big fight during the holidays. (Isn't that normal yet?)

These disruptive and frustrating events can become defining experiences on our path to peace. When our expectations aren't met and when the plans we had for an experience do not come into being, it forces us to ask the question:

Do we take control externally or surrender control internally?

Do we try and force reality into the shape of our expectations, or do we let go of our expectations and embrace the shape of what is? Do we fight, get angry, and manipulate everything around us until it looks the exact way we thought it was supposed to, or do we let the moment be exactly what it is, and let go of what we thought it was supposed to look like?

The brilliant Ilia Delio said, "We suffocate the life of the Spirit within us by controlling the space around us."

We can suffocate the Spirit, squeeze out joy, and push peace to the edge each time we try and control our space and force it to be something that it's not.

You cannot receive the peace of the moment when you need it to be something other than what it is.

It can feel like we are always going back to the garden insisting that we know the way, forcing things on our own terms, and stubbornly trying to cram the life of the infinite into our tiny, rigid, and laughable expectations.

But if you keep surrendering the particular way you think things are supposed to be, you keep opening up to the sacredness of the way things are, which gives you access to the peace that is present.

Have you ever had a bird shit on your ideal moment? Not metaphorically. I mean literally shit on your moment.

I have.

Let me explain.

It was a beautiful, gold, and glowing afternoon leading into the sunset. Due to my schedule that day, and the welcomed open space of time I had, I decided to pull into this massive empty parking lot and spend time in silence before I went home.

This is a special parking lot in our neighborhood because there is a giant Shepherd Fairey (the creator of OBEY) mural on one of the walls. One of the many perks of living in a neighborhood with one of the greatest street art events in the country every year.

So I pulled in and parked my car. I opened the trunk door, sat in the back, and had this deep sense something special was going to happen in this moment. I'm not sure what it was—maybe the Spirit would communicate something more specific than normal, perhaps some visual dynamic of the scene would speak some deep truth to my heart, I don't know.

But I had this sense of the sacred weight of the moment.

And then I looked up and saw a single bird sitting on a wire above me.

And as I fixed my gaze on it with the assumption or hope that something profound was going to take place, the bird took a huge shit. I could actually see the silhouette of the shit falling from the bird through the golden sky until it hit the ground.

Hilarious.

I came for Presence and peace, and was confronted by shit.

When this happened, I remember just smiling.

Was it what I expected? No. Was it what I envisioned? No. Was it what I hoped for? No. Was that the specific shape I thought the moment was going to have? Of course not.

But it was this quiet and comedic receiving of the situation for exactly what it was that allowed this less than ideal site to become another scene for the incarnation of Christ. I came to experience something profound and all I saw was a bird take a shit and fly away. And while the shape of the moment looked nothing like I wanted, the substance of Spirit was everything it's ever been.

The unexpected shit did not get in the way of the peace of the moment, it was the way to the peace in the moment.

Every time we surrender the particular shape of our preference, we enter into the universal flow of peace. The impulse of the ego is to mold each experience into a distinct shape that we believe will bring us peace. But the mystery is that the peace we desire comes from completely relinquishing and letting go of the need for our distinct desires to be achieved.

Our inability to release the specific pattern that we think we need in the moment is the very thing that gets in the way of settling into the sacred pattern that is always in place.

This is like refusing the gift because you do not like the way it's packaged.

Or missing out on water because you don't like the cup it's poured in.

Or missing out on the fire because of how the wood is arranged.

Learning to let go of the particular form that we believe will create peace opens us up to the universal flow of peace that is always flowing.

Even when there is unexpected shit you have to deal with.

My friends called me to remind me around 6:00 am that they were outside my place, and they were excited to go on the adventure we already planned.

I just woke up. It was kind of raining. And I was not quite as pumped up as they were for the excursion.

And by not quite as pumped up, I mean I did not want to go.

Two of my wife's and my best friends, Phil and Jen, were visiting Hawaii from Orange County, and on this specific morning, we planned on going swimming with the dolphins. I do not mean going to pay a ridiculous amount of money to put life vests on so we can pet a few dolphins being held in captivity. I mean going to a secret location on our island to swim off shore where pods of wild and free dolphins swim through every morning.

(And before you get the idea to message me, no, I cannot tell you where this is.)

So, we make the long drive (In Hawaii, anything over twenty to thirty minutes is long) and there's pockets of rain along the way, which keep reinforcing my lack of desire to do this. But we eventually arrive at our epic little location.

And right when we arrive, I could see the dolphins.

Now, this is a moment where I have seen countless people over the years fall into one of the strangest states I have ever witnessed in my life—I call it being dolphin drunk. It happens when the excitement of seeing dolphins in the wild creates an overflow of adrenaline, anticipation, and desire.

Basically, people get so excited they lose their minds and act drunk.

It's awesome to see, but it's also hazardous because of how it affects your decision making process.

So as we all adjust to our altered state of mind, we quickly grab our fins and masks, lock the car, and head to the water. We get to the shore and start to walk into the water and swim out. As I'm holding my mask in my hand, a small wave comes and crashes directly into my mask and pops out one of my lenses.

I look near my feet in the water.

It's gone.

It's not coming back.

Without lenses in a mask, you are unable to see anything underwater with clarity. So what that means is that while my friends are underwater having one of the most beautiful experiences possible, I will be treading water on the surface, and unable to be a part of it.

And while that happens, my friends are swimming out and getting ready to have the time of their lives with the other masks that I gave them.

My masks.

That I gave them.

And did I mention that I didn't really want to go that morning?

Now, I know what you're thinking.

"Oh, so you're not going to get to swim with dolphins with your precious little mask, how terribly tragic! You're in Hawaii. When we're talking about experiencing peace, this really isn't a big deal."

And I agree.

(Also I don't appreciate the tone.)

But I also know that the majority of the day to day things that rob you of your peace and get in the way of being in the divine flow are also not a big deal.

I know most of them are the small unmet expectations, the little frustrations when things don't go our way, the minor annoyances when people are violating simple forms of goodness, and when our own need for particularity is not actualized.

So, is me not being able to swim with dolphins with my mask some massive tragedy that is going to have grave social and economic implications for the community as a whole? Of course not.

But it is a good example of the uninvited disruptions that have the power to steal our peace—if we can't let go.

So while my friends were having one of the most mind blowing experiences of their lives, I could not be a part of it. And when it could have been so easy to get frustrated or feel sorry for myself because this experience did not turn out the way I wanted it to,

I just kind of laughed and let it go.

And as I floated on my back, missing out on the magic of being underwater with the dolphins, I formed my subtle smile of peace and thought,

when you are not grasping for anything, you discover you have everything.

Seven

WORKING FOR JUSTICE

In the mid-twentieth century south, Fannie Lou Hamer was one of the most fierce advocates for civil rights, and would go on to become one of the most out spoken and greatest freedom fighters in the history of the United States.

While Oscar Romero was a priest in El Salvador during one of the most brutal political regimes, he confronted and challenged the corrupt government again and again through the power of the Eucharist.

In the sixties and seventies, The Berrigan brothers, or "radical priests," as they were called by Time magazine, were an undeniable force in the peace movement. They even went so far as breaking into a government building and burning draft papers as a public demonstration against the war in Vietnam.

I could go on with a long list of names and voices who challenged the status quo, spoke truth to power, and gave their life to bear witness to Jesus' revolutionary vision of the Kingdom of God.

And what all of these voices have in common is that they did what they did because of the God they met in the Bible. They all believed that the Bible shows us God's imagination for compassion, justice and solidarity. Their lives kept insisting that we need to reclaim the Bible as a source of liberation and justice when it is too often used as a weapon for power and injustice.

But Fannie Lou Hamer was shot by the Ku Klux Klan, almost beaten to death by police, and faced constant resistance to her Jesus shaped vision of equality. Which are only a few of the reasons why she coined the phrase, "I'm sick and tired of being sick and tired."

After publicly providing the Eucharist and announcing the presence of God's nonviolent Kingdom after being told not to by the government, Fr. Oscar Romero was eventually assassinated while he was doing mass in El Salvador.

The Berrigan brothers were arrested around one hundred times for their public demonstrations and radical acts against injustice—even leading Daniel Berrigan to go underground in order to evade the FBI for an extended period of time.

These heroes of the Christian household inspire us through their relentless contribution to the good. They also show us the challenges of fighting for God's new world, have all felt the pain of taking Jesus' vision of the Kingdom of God seriously, and reveal the inevitability of coming face-to-face with the resistance of those in power.

Ilia Delio powerfully suggested that, "To be baptized is to give oneself wholeheartedly to this unfolding reality."

This is what these dreamers and pioneers have done with their lives that marks them as the saints and rebels of inspiration that they are.

They gave themselves to this world.

They poured their lives out as an offering for this world.

They carried the torch of justice through this world.

They dared to ask what if, in a world that is too comfortable living with the limitations of what is. Their voices emerged as the alarm clocks of justice ringing to wake people up, while most of the world ignored them and kept sleeping. They showed us the beauty of putting not just their thoughts on paper, but their bodies on the line as they stood their ground, held their signs, and moved their feet one step closer to that impossible dream of justice in the Kingdom of God.

These freedom fighters kept calling humanity beyond themselves, which we discovered was actually into ourselves. These are the ones that joined the march into God's future alongside those holy and reckless imagineers spoken of in that Hebrews 11 vision of this great cloud of witnesses.

And all of that sounds beautiful, poetic, and inspiring. (And it is.)

But those who have given their lives to care about justice and to fight against injustice know it is not that easy.

They know that to embrace the narrow path of visible resistance to the powers, you are going to know experiences of

heartbreak,

disappointment,

heaviness,

anger,

helplessness,

and are going to have as a companion the ongoing temptation to finally give up.

Or to stop giving yourself to the world.

Thankfully, what so many of these voices for justice show us in the later years of their life, is that you can keep caring and keep fighting for God's future without losing your hope. Their grounded presence and infectious laughter itself communicates that this work can be done while still maintaining a sense of humor, and living from the depths of the miracle of existence itself.

We can fight for justice without losing our joy.

Which of course, brings us back to the gong of remembering the heart of this book.

Letting go.

So what do we need to let go of while we are working and fighting for justice in order to maintain joy?

⁂

The first thing we need to let go of while pursuing justice and working for change is the need for things to change.

Perhaps, not what you were expecting me to begin with.

Maybe it initially seems counterintuitive or contradictory.

You might even think it doesn't make sense.

But stay with me.

There is a paradox at the heart of this work that not only empowers us to work for justice, but simultaneously liberates us to live with joy. This paradox is that letting go of the need for things to change is what places you in the best possible situation to create the change you desire, and to do so in a way that continuously changes you.

Moving forward is what inspires you to change the moment, but letting go is what allows the moment to change you.

And in the ongoing fight for justice, we need both.

For further clarity, when I write about letting go of the need for things to change, what I am referring to is the need of the ego for any social circumstances to change in order to be okay. Any time our ego or separate self demands or requires a specific outcome as a condition for happiness or peace, we give away our power and deny Spirit the power to be our unconditional source of life.

This is why when speaking of the desire to see people around us change, while letting go of the need for them to change, Richard Rohr writes, "Ironically, we are more than ever before in a position to change people—but we do not need to—and that makes all the difference."

All.

The.

Difference.

Not needing change is what makes all the difference while fighting for change.

Let's assume this is not only true of desiring to see individuals change, but also of the desire to see and work towards the change of systems of injustice as well.

What is the critical difference that not needing to change people or systems makes in our life while we are giving our lives to create this very change?

This difference is the primary determiner of whether or not we are going to experience

anger or acceptance,

frustration or freedom,

and whether or not we are going to be able to flow with the Spirit in the sacredness of the struggle itself.

This is why the smile and silliness of the Dalai Lama are so revolutionary. This is why the giggles and playfulness of Desmond Tutu are such powerful personal and political acts.

In his brilliant book, *The Book of Joy: Lasting Happiness in a Changing World*, Douglas Abrams profiles The Dalai Lama and Desmond Tutu, with an emphasis on how to live with joy. These are men who have lived under death threat for years of their lives and who have seen countless people they have loved killed during their struggle for justice and work for change.

The Dalai Lama even got kicked out of and exiled from his own country!

For perspective, I got banned from one Christian college campus here in Hawaii and it hurt me. He got kicked out of China!

These two compassionate men have faced the possibility of having their own lives taken from them. The same people they squeezed tightly and hugged out of love and solidarity during the struggle, they've had to let go of and entrust to the mystery of death. They have known every form of frustration, disappointment, and heartbreak as a result of their commitment to justice.

And yet, when they see each other, they giggle, tell inappropriate stories, and interrupt interviews because they're always tickling each other.

That freedom.

That joy.

That lightness.

That is the difference Rohr speaks of when he talks about how letting go of the need for change makes all the difference. I am convinced that letting go in the middle stages of your life is what allows you to laugh during the later stages of your life.

In our own struggle for justice, accompanied by the ever present need to let go, we need to understand there is a difference between overcoming and overcompensating.

Overcoming and overcompensating are not the same thing.

Let me begin with this.

Anything you do not overcome internally, you will overcompensate for externally.

Letting go of the ego need for things to change will require you to accept, transcend, and ultimately overcome some the most powerful illusions you may not even know you have. Often times, these illusions are what drive us into the work for justice, but if eventually not overcome, they can become the forces that destroy us while we are working for justice. What drives us into the struggle will often be what destroys us during the struggle.

We don't ever want any woman to experience being powerless again.

We refuse to allow any child to suffer under this unjust and oppressive system.

We are going to make sure no LGBTQ+ person has to know the pain of exclusion and rejection.

These desires inspire us and move us into the arena of life where we willingly put our lives on the line for the sake of others.

This is a good thing.

But as we give our lives to these individual causes in our universal pursuit of justice, we are eventually going to run into the inevitable walls of limitations.

No matter how hard we push, we meet more women who are living with that sense of powerlessness within the system we are fighting to eradicate.

As we endlessly give ourselves to change the economic and racist institutions in place, we keep seeing the damage done to children growing up in these conditions.

In the midst of us trying to inspire and organize in solidarity with the LGBTQ+ community, we are still seeing churches, workplaces, and families reject and deny the full humanity of queer people.

And now, when we run into these walls, this is where we are going to begin to meet, wrestle with, and hopefully overcome our own ego needs and illusions in the struggle.

As we face these walls of limitations, we sometimes respond by obsessively trying to control our environment to make sure no one ever has to feel powerless, or helpless, or rejected again.

We try to create a world that allows us to deny the truths we don't want to accept.

We do this as a way of denying the limitations we are being faced with, and as a way of avoiding confronting the illusions we have about the way life is supposed to work. If we were to confront our illusions and face some of our most feared truths about the way life works, it would be too painful and traumatic.

By the way, this impossible task of trying to control everything, fight everyone, and hold it altogether can drive us to exhaustion, and leave us feeling like we are constantly running on a stationary treadmill with no way to get off.

This is why we burnout.

This why we get angry and bitter.

This is why we feel like we are always fighting and never quite winning.

Overcompensating feels like we are endlessly fighting harder, moving faster, and holding together all of life itself. And we can keep doing this. The problem is that no matter how much good we accomplish while maintaining this pace, it is never going to be enough to overcome the illusions that are driving us beneath the surface. We can keep fighting and grinding in a way that almost kills us as we try and personally create a world where no person ever feels helpless or powerless again.

Or

We can accept a degree of powerlessness some people feel in our world.

We can befriend our limitations, transcend the part of us that can't embrace them, and be freed from the illusion that we can avoid them. Instead of overcompensating for our illusions externally, we can begin to come to terms with what they are internally. And when we do this, we can then return to the world and help those who are powerless, while knowing we cannot eliminate the presence of powerlessness as a whole. And we can embrace that it is not our individual responsibility to do so on our own.

This is a form of acceptance.

This is transcending our own illusions.

This is about coming to terms with shape of reality.

There's a story about this powerful young woman who was emerging as a leading voice for justice in our country. Not only was she a spellbinding communicator when it came to speaking of a more just world, she was a relentless activist working to create a more just world.

She was leading this new era of prophetic fire and activism.

During this meteoric rise, she was leading an organization focused on empowering BIPOC leaders in the arts, she had published her first book, and was becoming one of the most sought after speakers at conferences and events.

Her presence felt unstoppable and her commitment seemed unshakable.

But right around the time her second book was coming out, she started getting sick more frequently. She was having a hard time sleeping because of the attacks from others. Due to the the adrenaline and anxiety of her pace of life, after all these years, the fire inside began to feel like fumes.

She finally broke down. She refused last minute to show up to a big speaking engagement, felt like she was unable to leave her home, and started this long journey of coming to terms with the real fragile emotional state she was in.

And after countless conversations with close friends, hours and hours of sitting with her therapist, and time to just be, she finally had this jarring realization,

"No matter how hard I fight, I cannot stop all of the suffering. No matter how much I do, I cannot eradicate all pain from this world...I've been fighting to alleviate pain in this world for so long because I've been unable to accept pain as an inevitable part of this world and my own life."

Was the work this young woman was doing in this world good? Of course. She was driven by her compassion and a real desire to overcome pain with love and create a better world for others.

But, what she eventually discovered was that her drive was not only about alleviating pain for others, it was also about avoiding the reality of pain herself. While all of the energy she gave was celebrated because of the good it created for others, it was also a form of her overcompensating for some of the illusions she was carrying.

She thought it was possible to never have to feel any form of pain.

She thought if she worked hard enough, no young people would ever have to face the pain she faced growing up.

She thought she could save everyone she advocated for.

Those are illusions.

There's a difference between dying to something, and that thing killing you. We can almost kill ourselves trying to convince ourselves that an illusion is true. We can be killed by the illusions we are trying to keep alive. Or we can die to our illusions and be able to live.

We do not need to overcompensate while we work against injustice, we need to overcome our illusions during the process.

And when we do this, we are mysteriously liberated to keep working for justice and change in a way where our life is not contingent on the outcomes.

We no longer need to overcompensate externally for things we have overcome internally.

The second thing we have to let go of in our journey toward justice is the need for power.

In Mark 9, Jesus was walking with the disciples through Galilee and talking to them about the future, about his suffering, about power, and about the holy pattern of crucifixion and resurrection.

And almost immediately after this, the disciples started arguing about who was going to be the greatest and who was going to have the most power.

This is the moment where I believe Jesus invented the facepalm.

Jesus keeps talking about giving his life, surrendering power, and about his lack of a need for status. And his disciples are still arguing over who is going to have the highest degree of the very kind of power and status he cares nothing about.

(Here's the thing: the disciples are just a reflection of the culture they were living in. Where status is everything, where power is dominating, and everything is about your cultural image and what social position in society you have, they are simply an uncritical reflection of their culture.

Can you believe there were disciples arguing over power, status, and fame?

Now we have a church where people use each other to get ahead, where people name drop to seem more important, that believes being on a stage or performing in front of crowds is the highest achievement you can get, and we've created an entire culture of church that thinks being on stage in front of a crowd is the ultimate expression of God's work, blessing and affirmation. Seems that we are still reflecting the cultural status quo as well.

We are always critical of the disciples, and yet we are always still having these same conversations.)

There is this great story about Jesus, power, and kids.

They came to Capernaum. When he was in the house, he asked them, "What were you arguing about on the road?" But they kept quiet because on the way they had argued about who was the greatest.

Sitting down, Jesus called the Twelve and said, "Anyone who wants to be first must be the very last, and the servant of all."

He took a little child whom he placed among them. Taking the child in his arms, he said to them, "Whoever welcomes one of these little children in my name welcomes me; and whoever welcomes me does not welcome me but the one who sent me."

While the disciples are arguing about power, position and who is the greatest, Jesus places a child right in front of them and completely changes the conversation.

Jesus takes a child with no status, no power, and no position, and Jesus lifts this kid up as if to say,

this is real power.

Power?

Huh?

This is power?

Really?

How is one of the most economically vulnerable and politically fragile people in their society somehow supposed to teach them anything about power?

Here is a little secret to this story.

This is peak satire Jesus.

This is the fullness of divine energy as this first-century Palestinian prophet and provocateur making fun of their notion of power. Jesus is mocking the power they are so seduced by. Jesus is laughing at their cultural ideas of power. Jesus is allowing this powerless child to ask this powerful question:

"Do you really take any of that posturing and lame sense of status seeking seriously?"

What is on display is the Christ shaped form of power that comes from not needing any power. (At least what we usually think of as power.)

Jesus is essentially and brilliantly mocking all cultural definitions of power and exposing the emptiness of the relentless pursuit of positions. Jesus reveals something quite unique and surprising.

Real power comes from not caring about power at all.

We crave power because we think it eliminates the possibility of pain, protects us from vulnerability, ensures that we are going to win, and guarantees we will always be on top. Jesus turns our notion of power on in its head by revealing the freedom of befriending pain, embracing vulnerability, and completely doing away with any ego need to win.

This is why we have to talk about Amy Schumer, Kanye West, and Kim Kardashian.

Amy Schumer tells one of the greatest red carpet stories of all time. She was walking the red carpet for The Time 100 Gala, and describes one of the most legendary interactions with Kim and Kanye.

As she explains how this story unfolded during a later interview, she says,

"I think falling is the funniest thing in the world."

"I'm on the red carpet and feel stupid...they're just humiliating anyway."

While doing an interview she says, "They didn't want to interview me...they thought I was Adele."

And she goes on to say, "Kim and Kanye were working it and being all short and important and they're like, "You're Welcome!"

And after the reflection, humiliation, and just overall sense of how silly the whole red carpet experience is, she turns to her publicist and says, ""Can I fall in front of them?"

That is when she decides she needs to run over, pretend to trip, and throw her body right in front of Kanye West and Kim Kardashian, while grunting out "uuuugghhhhh" as if she just got bitten by a shark.

And she did it.

And when it happened, Kanye West just looked disgusted and walked away.

So ridiculous and hilarious.

But here's the brilliance of that moment.

Amy Schumer was doing the same thing when she fell on the red carpet that Jesus was doing when he placed that child in front of him. They're both saying, "Do you really take all this seriously? Do you really want this? Can't you see this posturing and obsession with status is a joke? This isn't real. This doesn't matter."

Her foolishness exposed the foolishness of the whole thing. Her making fun of herself was actually her making fun of the entire culture of celebrity, status, and the desire for power as a whole. Her not taking herself seriously and being ridiculous, was her saying none of this should be taken seriously and it's all ridiculous.

Jesus and Amy Schumer both show us that

the moment you discover that you do not need that kind of power, is the moment you realize how powerful you really are.

What the culture around us sees as power, Jesus sees as nothing. We don't need to endlessly maneuver to put ourselves in positions of power. We don't have to use the tools of the oppressors or the instruments of the insecure systems around us to build for the Kingdom of God. We don't have to try and leverage every single relationship to climb some ladder to the top that has a view that looks nothing like Jesus' vision of justice. We don't need to seek out platforms that have been constructed for shows and performances to put the truth on display.

And as we let go of these things while we are courageously pursuing justice, we just might make room for all of the joy along the way.

Eight
ACCEPTANCE

The cross is an icon of acceptance.

Jesus was born out of the human experience by, as, and for love. He revealed himself as a healer to anyone, a friend to everyone, and a defender of the marginalized. He took the time to care for individuals, spent time at parties and dinners enjoying life with larger groups, and spoke truth to power and challenged evil and injustice at institutional levels.

He was literally love incarnate, the universal drive toward justice, and the cosmic glue that holds together the entire cosmos. And the one who also sits down at the banquet table of the universe inviting all of humanity to take a seat.

And he was killed.

Well, first he was questioned, misunderstood, doubted, criticized, mocked, betrayed, abandoned, beaten, and laughed at.

Then he was killed.

At one point near the end of the excruciating process leading toward his death, while suffering on the cross, Jesus said,

"Father, forgive them, for they do not know what they are doing."

Which, like always, raises all kinds of interesting questions: Who are they and them? The individuals crucifying him? The criminals who are being crucified next to him? All of humanity at that time? Or is he giving us a vision of his heart for the historical and universal family of humanity itself, because of what we keep doing to each other and ended up doing to him?

While asking the Father for forgiveness, he is showing us the path of acceptance.

He does not argue with the Father about whether or not what is happening to him is fair. You do not see Jesus fighting reality or resisting what is happening as a protest against the way the world is supposed to treat you when you give so much love. And He refuses to scapegoat, blame, or hate anyone or anything while he is in the middle of receiving hate and blame and being scapegoated himself.

He miraculously allows everything to be exactly what it is, embraces everyone into him with all of their darkness, and speaks this life altering word of forgiveness and universal acceptance.

Acceptance is at the center of what was happening on the cross.

Which is strange, since people don't talk about it very much.

Cynthia Bourgeault, in her singular work, *The Wisdom Jesus,* offers one of the most enlightening words on the nature of acceptance and darkness embedded in the death of Christ. She writes,

He was just sitting there—surrounded by the darkest, deepest, most alienated, most constricted states of pained consciousness; sitting if we can imagine it, among all those mirroring faces of the collective false self that we encountered earlier in the crucifixion narrative: the anguish of Judas, the indecision of Pilate, the cowardice of Peter, the sanctimony of the Pharisees; sitting there in *the midst of all this blackness, not judging, not fixing, **just letting it be in love**.*

And in so doing, he was allowing love to go deeper, pressing all the way to the innermost ground out of which the opposites arise and holding on to that light. A quiet, harmonizing love was infiltrating even the deepest places of darkness and blackness, in a way that didn't override them or cancel them, but gently reconnected them to the whole.

"...not judging, not fixing, just letting it be in love."

"...he was allowing love to go deeper..."

"...in a way that didn't override them or cancel them, but gently reconnected them to the whole."

This is why the cross is an icon of not only acceptance, but of reality itself.

Jesus reveals that there is no resurrection without death, and there is no death without acceptance. Jesus is taking each step of the full human journey, and in doing so, surprisingly uncovers that acceptance is at the heart of the human experience. He exposes that the love that flows through acceptance into the darkest and scariest places within us, actually fills them, invites them to join in the unity of all things, and reconnects them to the whole.

Which is why Bourgeault goes on to say that it was "...in that great gesture of self surrender through which the world was redeemed."

Acceptance is what re-connects the parts of you that are separate.

Acceptance is what transforms anger into joy.

Acceptance is what makes the path of healing possible.

Acceptance is the threshold we cross to enter into the reunion between the presence of God and the wholeness of our humanity.

Acceptance is the container that holds the past and present, darkness and light, joy and pain, and shakes them up and transforms them all into One thing.

Years ago, a good friend of mine got hired as the young adults pastor for a megachurch in Texas. This was one of those classic suburban megachurches where the pastor is basically a CEO, the bottom line of the church is "butts in seats and bucks in the plate," almost everyone is white, and everything that truly matters happens on a huge stage with perfectly placed lights.

You know?

Like the exact way Jesus intended.

(I laughed as I wrote that.)

After wrestling with a pastoral calling for years, he finally decided to take the leap and start his pastoral work with this church.

This was it.

He took this courageous risk to be faithful to his calling.

Finally, the moment came.

He was risking. He was trusting. He was doing it.

And they let him go in just two years.

My friend was devastated. And when he was having his final conversations with staff in the church, they talked about the numbers of kids who were showing up (like I said, butts in seats), and other vague spiritual things about where God was leading them. And ultimately, that they were deciding to release him.

Very short.

Very business like.

Very matter of fact.

At the same time while this was happening to my friend, the church was in the middle of this massive renovation project. This project meant a multi-million dollar atrium, fresh build outs around campus, and a brand new million dollar screen for the sanctuary.

You know?

Like the kind Jesus always dreamt of us having.

First, my friend is hurt because of how much he sacrificed and gave to the church and to the people he cared for, only to be let go because he wasn't living up to their cultural and corporate expectations. Then second, after being told they were unwilling to pay his annual salary (which was essentially an unlivable wage), he finds out they are spending around four-hundred-thousand dollars each to get other brand new screens for the sanctuary that already had massive screens that worked fine.

My friend was so faithful and gave so much. And they let him go.

Okay. Let's fast forward to the hot tub.

About a year and a half after being let go, my friend was visiting us in Hawaii. On one of his last days here, we were sitting in a hot tub together in the middle of the day talking about what happened. And as he was sharing about the process, he started to choke up and express his emotions because clearly he was still hurt.

(Just two straight white guys in a hot tub in the middle of a Tuesday crying. Something about that is hilarious to me.)

What was happening through those tears was not only the expression of the hurt, but the movement toward the full acceptance of what happened to him. It wasn't just him talking about what happened, it was him getting closer to coming to terms with and accepting what happened. He was right there on the edge of breaking through the walls of resistance and transitioning into acceptance.

He was so close.

It was like he walked right up to the door of acceptance where it was time to let go and be freed from the anger, and as he started to turn the knob and the emotions started to flow, I could see him pull back and stay where he was. Right before he crossed over the threshold of acceptance, he uttered some dismissive phrase like, "it's all good," pulled back from the emotions, cutting off the fullness of feeling his way all the way through. In that moment, he remained on the doorstep of acceptance, never fully crossing over that threshold.

There was something about what happened that was too painful to accept.

There was something he was holding onto that he wasn't ready to let go of.

He started to feel the weight of reality, and when it came time to cross over the threshold into acceptance, he decided it was too much, turned around, and stayed where he was.

It is so interesting that he did that.

And even more interesting how we can all do that sometimes.

Why did my friend step back when he got so close? What is it about acceptance that is so scary? Why is acceptance so painful? What is happening during that unique environment of acceptance that makes it one of the most difficult things for us to do?

Well.

Acceptance is always connected to death.

Actually.

Acceptance is death.

Acceptance is always a funeral for our ideals, expectations, and illusions.

It's giving up our security blanket and walking into an unfamiliar room with strangers. It's stripping off our armor as we prepare for war. It's laying down our weapons in what feels like the apex of the battle. It's knocking down the walls that you have stayed behind for protection your entire life. It's being pushed on to stage naked in front of a crowd with no way to escape.

Or, at least that's how it feels to us right before we do it.

This is why we avoid it, distract ourselves from it, and convince ourselves the solution to our problem is always a million other things than the one thing it usually is.

We struggle with acceptance because we just aren't very good at dying and letting go.

In a different part of her book, *The Wisdom Jesus,* Bourgeault goes on to say,

"We wish God could be only light. We wish the world could be only light. We wish that darkness and evil and cruelty would vanish, and we keep trying to work our way back up the great chain of being by rejecting the darkness and cleaving to the light."

In other words, there are parts of life we are simply unwilling to accept.

We don't want to accept that life isn't fair.

We don't want to accept that sometimes the people who are supposed to love you well are not going to.

We don't want accept that love is always a risk and that there are no guarantees.

We don't want to accept that we can do everything right and try so hard to be good, and things still might not work out.

We don't want to accept the flaws and imperfections in others or ourselves.

We don't want to accept that some parts of our story are actually a part of our story.

But without the letting go of the way we thought life was supposed to be, we will never be able to embrace how beautiful life truly is. This is why understanding the cross as an icon of acceptance is so central to Jesus, and so powerful for us.

The cross is God's way of still speaking to humanity and saying,

"Accept it. Trust it. Feel it. Let it go. It's going to be okay."

Sometimes real faith in The Christ hanging on the cross of acceptance, is trusting that somehow you will be carried through safely to the other side of your own acceptance.

Jesus forgave humanity for what they did and we have to forgive others for what they've done. Jesus embraced the darkness present in his own experiences and we have to embrace the darkness in ours too. Jesus accepted the unfair nature of life as he was betrayed, mocked, and crucified by the ones he loved, and we have to accept that life is unfair through betrayals, and the many deaths along the way.

Acceptance is the ultimate act of trust in God.

Leading into the end of 2016 was one of the hardest chapters of my life while pastoring. I just experienced our first major relational loss when one of the best friends who was helping lead left the church, and essentially ended our friendship. My wife and I were about to have our first child, and ninety percent of our income from the first few years of planting the church was about to be gone.

Our community was in this weird and awkward shift where many of the familiar faces were gone, and a flood of new and unfamiliar faces were now occupying their place. And on top of all of that, we had about a month left in the year and had no place for our church to meet when the new year began.

Oh yeah, and barely any money in the church's bank account.

Every pillar that held up my personal, relational, economic, and social life felt like it was breaking. I had every reason to allow the pressure of my circumstances to lead me to anger, frustration, or to throw a pity party for myself. (Which one tactic of the ego to hold on to power that I am particularly drawn to.)

"How could you lead me here God when I gave up everything for you?"

"I've done everything with integrity and never sold out and became another used car salesman, celebrity obsessed pastor, and this is where it gets me?"

"I've let go of so much money from outside sources to ensure that I can preach with authenticity and honesty, and I don't even know how I can afford to pay rent two months after my first kid is born."

These were the convulsions of my contracted ego during this challenging season.

But the one defining thing that protected me from acting out of fear and anxiety, from getting bitter and resentful, or from giving up and shutting my heart down was acceptance.

That's it. The one thing that kept me and grounded me was acceptance.

I simply embraced the season with all of its struggles and that chapter of my life with all of its challenges. In those moments, where my ego contracts and tries to convince me to feel sorry for myself or to just silently check out, this larger and deeper Self throws its arms wide open and envelops everything exactly as it is, and trusts the Christ of universal acceptance.

Acceptance is about befriending reality, no matter what she looks like in the moment.

This is why in the last chapter of his life, and after going through degrees of suffering most people cannot even fathom, the Archbishop Desmond Tutu says, "Acceptance—whether we believe in God or not—allows us to move into the fullness of joy."

Always.

Always.

Always.

Acceptance always leads us to joy.

Acceptance is when we are arguing, clinging, fighting, and trying to maintain control of the way we want the world to be, and then listen to the gentle whisper of the Spirit saying, "but it's not that way, and that's okay," until we finally collapse into her arms that alone can carry us forward.

Acceptance transcends the dualistic mind, and aligns our mind, heart, and bodies in a Christlike way of being in the world. It allows us to embrace death and affirm life in the exact same moment.

Acceptance is about looking at the moment in all of her wild and untamed energy, and weeping over the fact that she's not who you thought she was, then discovering that she is more beautiful than you could have ever imagined.

Acceptance is the deep personal experience of knowing that you don't have to hold onto anything when you know you are being held by everything. (I know I say that a lot.)

With all of that said, what does acceptance have to do with letting go?

Everything.

Because acceptance always comes before letting go.

Nine

WELCOME AND INCLUSION

To be invited, included and welcomed are some of the most meaningful experiences you can have as a human being.

Also,

to be ignored, excluded, and rejected are some the most devastating experiences you can have.

Just recently I got an email that had an immediate impact on me. The name in the quick alert I got on my phone was someone whose book is sitting in a prominent place on my book shelf. I read the email and it was an invitation to a rooftop event in New York City that was going to be lead by him and many other voices who I respect.

The invite itself meant so much to me.

Being invited by him and included in this experience made an impression on me like I was being invited by the Spirit and included in something special in the universe as a whole.

An invitation is always more than an invitation, and being welcomed is always more than being welcomed.

To be invited into a particular place feels like an invitation in a more universal space. To be welcomed by a concrete group of people registers in our soul as a more cosmic welcoming into life itself. Being included at the specific table set by people with care is to further trust that you are included by God at the banquet table of the universe set by love itself.

Haven't you ever felt this?

A new opportunity arises and somehow makes you feel like all is right in the world. The recognition of connection, the feeling of being embraced, and the power of being seen by a group of people become the very experience of being seen, known, and embraced by God. A personal invitation that is meaningful to you gets through to your heart in a way that makes you feel more at home in this world as a whole.

Yes!

Because an invitation is always more than an invitation, and being welcomed is always more than being welcomed.

If this is true in the good sense when you are on the receiving end of invitation, inclusion, and welcome, it is just as true in the hard sense when you are on the other side of these as well.

The ignoring, rejection, and the exclusion feel like they are coming from the width of the universe and hit us in the depth of our souls. On a personal level, rejection from a community becomes the experience of being rejected by life. Being marginalized or shut out from a desired group can feel like being pushed to the edges of the entire universe.

There's a story about this sexually questioning young woman and her mother. While being confused about her sexuality for years, and going on the long process of understanding herself and coming to terms with her desires, she was finally in a place to tell her parents that she was a lesbian.

In the midst of all the anxiety, the deafening pounding of her heart, and the catastrophic fear of how her traditionally evangelical parents were going to react, she sat down with both of them and told them she thought she was a lesbian.

Her father cried, but stayed there with her.

Her mother did not say a word and just left the room and barely spoke to her again for years.

She said that when her mom left, it felt like God and His love left the room too. Her mom leaving registered emotionally as if God Himself left the room, exited her life, and took any possibility of being loved with him.

This is because exclusion is always more than exclusion, and rejection is always more than rejection.

Here's the good news. Jesus was the most welcoming and inclusive person in human history, and the original fire set by the church was one that burned bright with the flames of inclusion.

In Luke 8:40-47, Jesus has this mind bending sequence of events with a religious leader, his daughter, and a notoriously "unclean" woman. Here is the beginning of the story.

Now when Jesus returned, a crowd welcomed him, for they were all expecting him. Then a man named Jairus, a synagogue leader, came and fell at Jesus' feet, pleading with him to come to his house because his only daughter, a girl of about twelve, was dying.

As Jesus was on his way, the crowds almost crushed him. And a woman was there who had been subject to bleeding for twelve years, but no one could heal her. She came up behind him and touched the edge of his cloak, and immediately her bleeding stopped.

"Who touched me?" Jesus asked.

When they all denied it, Peter said, "Master, the people are crowding and pressing against you."

But Jesus said, "Someone touched me; I know that power has gone out from me."

Then the woman, seeing that she could not go unnoticed, came trembling and fell at his feet. In the presence of all the people, she told why she had touched him and how she had been instantly healed. Then he said to her, "Daughter, your faith has healed you. Go in peace."

So, this story begins with Jairus, a synagogue leader, whose role it was to maintain the reading of the law and the keeping of the commandments. Jairus was a hyper religious man. This is a person who knows the law inside and out, and who has embraced a role of not only maintaining the law himself, but of watching to make sure other people follow the law as well.

And this religious man comes to Jesus because he was desperate for his daughter to be healed.

While they are now on the way to this man's house so Jesus can heal his daughter, another woman comes up to Jesus, touches his cloak and gets healed, and eventually throws herself at his feet in fear and trembling.

The story said this woman had been bleeding for twelve years. This flow of blood, or *"rhysis haimatos,"* comes from Leviticus 15:25-27, and was a term used for vaginal bleeding outside of your period. Since this kind of bleeding would have made a woman ceremonially "unclean," the fact that this woman was bleeding for twelve years would have left her in a perpetual state of impurity to the people in her tribe.

This would have made the woman ritually unclean for 12 years, which means she would not have had right relationship with the community, the synagogue, or the village for 12 years. This woman was seen as being as dirty, unwelcomed, disruptive, and unclean as it gets.

Twelve years of rejection.

Twelve years of isolation.

Twelve years of loneliness.

This would have been unbelievably destructive for her on a personal and social level.

No one was allowed to touch her.

No one would remain in her presence.

No prophet or healer would ever go near this woman.

If they did, they would be considered unclean as well, which would have had serious consequences because of the Law.

And despite all of this, after being touched by her, Jesus tells her, "Daughter, your faith has healed you. Go in peace."

(Which is also the only place in all of the gospels he uses this intimate term daughter, for anyone.)

Jesus, being touched by an unclean woman, ignored any social boundaries of impurity from the Law, and completely subverted the expectations of the teachers of the Law. The disciples would have been embarrassed, uncomfortable, and ashamed. They would have been left wondering if this was okay, or anxious about what others thought who saw this event. They'd be asking,

"Does God do this?"

"Does Jesus do this?"

"Is this okay?"

"Can we do this?"

People would see this and judge Jesus, question his leadership, and accuse him of disobeying God and the Temple. And in the center of all of the confusion, judgment and internal debates about what God is okay with, Jesus boldly steps in, cuts through the noise, extends compassion, and provides healing.

This story began with the father Jairus, a synagogue leader, whose role it was to maintain the keeping of the commandments, asking Jesus to heal his daughter. It ended with Jesus breaking the father's own commandments to heal others on the way to heal his own daughter.

The freedom of Jesus and the brilliance of the gospel writers are amazing.

And when Jesus refers to her as daughter, he not only heals her, he pronounces her clean, restoring her to the community as well. Not only is she healed by Jesus, but she is to be welcomed by the people. So in the end, Jesus essentially says, "I broke your laws to heal her, and now you're going to accept her."

See, you can be an outsider to the religious system, but you are never an outsider to Christ.

Too many people are accepted by God, but don't know it because they haven't been embraced by the church. When churches say they are welcoming of everyone, I believe they are sincere in their intentions, but I also know they don't always know how to make this intention into a lived reality.

But this is who we are. We are the welcomers of people into the heart of life and the center of God.

We get to include people with a kind of love that allows them to trust for the first time that they are included in God. Our welcome of people in the church has the power to help them feel welcome in the universe as a whole. Cultivating a space where people can truly feel at home in the body of Christ becomes a part of people learning how to feel at home in their own bodies.

In the name of the Father, Son, and Holy Spirit, we are to live lives of welcome, acceptance, and grace.

So why is it so hard to unconditionally love and include people who are different? Why do so many churches say everyone is welcome and yet reveal again and again how impossible it is for them to actually live this out? Why do we personally get uncomfortable when certain kinds of people are welcomed, included, or close to us?

Or perhaps the best question is: what do we have to let go of in order to welcome and include others?

The first thing we need to let go of to become more welcoming and inclusive is the need to control other people's journey.

About twenty-five of us were gathered around our table and trying to squeeze into the kitchen to pray together before we started dinner. This is an intentional moment we always had on these nights to remind people about being present, about waking up to the miracle of the mundane, and how the entire mystery of the universe is packed into this kitchen in the midst of all of us.

Right when we were quieting down and about pray, Cali—this young and vibrant El Salvadorian young man from Los Angeles—took out a forty ouncer of Colt 45 and placed it in the middle of the table we were all gathered around.

(By the way, if you didn't grow up drinking malt liquor like we did, Colt 45 is a staple in this legacy.)

Here is this gathering for our new church, and right before the prayer begins, when everyone's attention is focused, he busts out his forty and just puts it on display for all to see. Which by the way, I suspected was not his first forty of the night!

So, what was my early pastoral response to this?

Of course, I did the one thing that made sense. I asked Cali to be the one to pray for dinner.

Although at first, he resisted because he had never prayed in public before, I put him on the spot, and he finally gave in. And when he did, he prayed this hilarious, honest, and heartfelt prayer, and then the night moved on and we started to eat.

A little while later, as I was pouring myself a glass of wine, Cali walked up to where the drinks were, because apparently it was time for him to transition from malt liquor to white wine. Right when he came up, I smiled and said, "I know you were testing people when you did that."

He kind of laughed a little, but got serious and responded with, "I ain't gonna lie. I was testing people. I don't know these people. Kev, I know you accept me as I am, but I don't know about everyone else. And plus, you said I could be accepted here for me, and if this was a Wednesday night and I was at my place, I would be drinking this forty. So if I can be accepted for me here, well, this is me."

In that defining moment, I specifically asked him to pray because I knew that he was testing people. He was seeing if he was right in his assumption that they were going to judge him, reject him, or get uncomfortable when he did that. I needed him and everyone else who was a part of our church in the beginning to see that

the moment he thought he was going to be excluded, he was included.

The moment he thought he would be rejected, he was welcomed.

And the moment he assumed his voice would be devalued or silenced, it was actually elevated in the community and celebrated by the church as he prayed.

Deciding to respond the way I did was me saying to the community, whatever you think about what it means to be embraced and welcomed by the church needs to be let go of if you're going to be a part of building this new thing. You have ideas about how you're supposed to behave in church that need to be let go of for us to become a place defined by that boundary breaking, Christ shaped hospitality in the gospels. You have mental categories of how to decide when and where a person is acceptable to God that need to be surrendered.

The very space that is supposed to be known by its faith, hope, and love has become a place that is too often known for its fear, judgment, and hypocrisy. And to be a truly welcoming community, we have to get over our need to control people and their process.

Henri Nouwen wrote, "To die to our neighbors means to stop judging them, to stop evaluating them, and thus to become free to be compassionate."

To which I would add, also free to be loving, inclusive, welcoming, and accepting.

Our job is to free people to encounter God authentically, not shame them to follow rules superficially. An inclusive community has no boundaries to keep people out, but it does have something compelling at the center which draws people in. There are no gatekeepers and law makers turning people away, because everyone is perpetually invited to move closer to the center, which is Christ.

This is why my questions for religious people specifically who spend energy worrying about who is being embraced:

What does what they're doing have to do with what you're experiencing?

Or

What does their behavior have to do with your ability to find life?

When we are focused on what others are doing with their life, we miss out on what God is doing in our life. When I see people judging others, I see people who, on some level, still struggle with feeling judged. When I see people refusing to give grace to others, I see people who probably have a really hard time experiencing grace and trusting in their own value. When I see people judging others, I see people who do not know for themselves how good God actually is and how valuable they are.

Judgment is us telling people who they aren't, and grace is us trusting in who we are.

We can let go of the burden of controlling other people's journeys and not only free them up to experience God and life more deeply, but free ourselves up to do the same.

The next things we need to let go of in order to be more inclusive is our antiquated ideas about people being clean and unclean, and the need to decide who is in and who is out.

A young woman who was relatively new to our church came out for the first time publicly right before she entered the water to get baptized. It was amazing to see how the love and inclusion of the church was the very welcoming of her over the threshold into the love and inclusion of God.

I have a running joke with a woman in Imagine who works in design and finds herself drawn to the contemplative stream of spirituality. I always say to her, "The less certain you get of your beliefs about Jesus, the more free you become in Christ."

This guy who had gotten out of prison and was coming to church for the first time used to tell me he would be tracking with me so much as I preached, but whenever I said the name Jesus, it would throw him off and confuse him. And yet, I could see the Spirit breaking him down, clearing the way, and preparing him for a new future. Even without the name of Jesus, the presence of Christ was changing him.

In the early years of Imagine while we were still meeting in our house, I preached about the power of being seen by God. During communion, I looked to my porch and saw a young person from our church sitting down who wasn't there before that, and when I looked up again, he was gone. I went outside and found him walking, and he turns around and says, "I'm not gonna lie, I'm on mushrooms right now. And I'm just on a journey walking around. But I came here and felt like God wanted me to tell you that He sees you." And then he just walked off into the night with a smile on his face.

One Sunday morning during worship and storytelling between songs, a young local girl shares about her experience at the church being welcomed and feeling at home as an LGBTQ person, and when I look out to the crowd, I see another young LGBTQ girl who has never stepped foot in our church before with tears streaming down her face.

I remember a more conservative middle aged man listening to a story like this one morning, having never heard an LGBTQ+ person share in front of a church, and he asked, "Can you do this?"

In all these stories, who is clean and unclean? Which of these people is in and which ones are out? Who is the real Christian? The young, LGBTQ kid who doesn't believe in Jesus, but is experiencing the Spirit? Or the middle aged man who believes in Jesus but is having a hard time experiencing the Spirit present in that space? Who is really "saved?"

Or perhaps the more important question is, are these even helpful questions?

We believe strongly and then begin to doubt. We know we have experienced the presence of God, but we aren't sure what to believe about God. We are intrigued by and even committed to Christ, but still have so many questions. We want to go all in but there are all kinds of cultural and religious barriers that are usually getting in the way. We know we are unconditionally embraced by God, but still broadly rejected and excluded by the church.

Traveling the way of Jesus is more of a faith process than a finished product.

And faith is always a process because life is always a process.

We keep focusing on giving people answers, conclusions, and trying to get them in. Jesus seemed more interested in questions, a path, and trying to help move people forward.

There's a famous and simple story about Jesus around a dinner table.

In Mark 2:15-17, the gospel writer notes,

While Jesus was having dinner at Levi's house, many tax collectors and sinners were eating with him and his disciples, for there were many who followed him. When the teachers of the law who were Pharisees saw him eating with the sinners and tax collectors, they asked his disciples: "Why does he eat with tax collectors and sinners?"

On hearing this, Jesus said to them, "It is not the healthy who need a doctor, but the sick. I have not come to call the righteous, but sinners."

In this story, the religious authorities and gatekeepers are upset and offended that Jesus is eating with certain people. And it is not just that the keepers of the law were uncomfortable with some of these people personally, it was that these people who were sharing this intimate space with Jesus were considered ceremonially unclean. And if they were ceremonially unclean, then by proximity, that would now mean that Jesus was unclean.

These people were outsiders who did not belong to their tribe. They hadn't performed the rituals, they didn't have the right beliefs, and if Jesus were a good Jew, he would have corrected them and removed himself from that setting.

They questioned Jesus because they believed they were defending God.

They saw Jesus' inclusion of them as an actual offense to God.

The law they were upholding from God did not give Jesus the permission to love like God.

For them, there were clear categories of clean and unclean, in and out, accepted and rejected, included and excluded, and they believed it was their religious obligation to not only maintain these lines, but to constantly decide who was in which category.

This is what is called religion as discrimination.

Or

Spirituality by elimination.

But in the gospels, Jesus radically reframes notions of clean and unclean, and inclusion and exclusion. Rather than focusing on "unclean" people, Jesus focuses on the boundaries separating clean from unclean and says, "That's whats evil." The separating boundary itself is the problem, and the entire system that perpetuates the ideas of clean and unclean is what's evil.

This is why Richard Beck, in his brilliant book, *Unclean,* wrote, "Transgressing boundaries is integral to the act of embrace." The problem is never the people on the other side of the boundaries, the problem is the internalized power of the boundary itself.

Those people are not the problem, the way you see those people is the problem. What's sinful is not the people on the other side of the line, what's sinful is the line itself. What's sinful is not the people rejected by the system, what's sinful is the very religious system that is doing the rejecting. What's sinful is not the people who we exclude from within our boundaries, what's sinful is the exclusionary boundaries themselves. What's sinful is not who ever is out when we decide who is in and who is out, whats sinful is the very spirit that spends all of its energy worrying about whose in and whose out.

Love dismantles all of the boundaries that separate us.

Including the ones you believe were set in place by God.

As long as we are obsessing over or spending our energy protecting boundaries (which don't exist), defending God (who doesn't need it), making our cases for who is clean and unclean (which aren't even valid categories), or standing up for God's laws (which are nothing in the presence of God's love), we do not get to witness these beautiful stories the Spirit is writing through lives of the people you believe are outside.

If you find yourself spending more energy worrying about who is being welcomed and accepted by the church than spending time with people that are seen as outsiders, you might be missing the whole thing.

Letting go of what we see as the exclusive rules of God's law has the power to make room for all of humanity to know the inclusive reality of God's love.

I remember when I first started seeing this young couple coming around Imagine more and more. One of the girls seemed familiar and comfortable with the Jesus thing. The other girl seemed stoic, distant, and like she really wanted to make her presence known as a young, strong woman who was there with her girlfriend, but not really into the whole church thing.

At some point in that season, I would see them start to stand up, hold hands, and come to the table and take communion together. Moments like that always made me so happy, and made me feel like pastoring made sense to me.

Fast forward a bit ahead in their journey, and a group of us from the church are gathered at the beach to support, celebrate, and be present to this young couple as they were getting baptized together. One of the girl's father was there with his girlfriend, and we were there praying, affirming them, and singing our way into the water.

But I found out later, there was another interesting scene taking place the night before.

A group of guys were sitting around a table, hanging out, and talking about what they thought about our church, and us as pastors for baptizing this young lesbian couple.

(For clarity, the guys involved I know personally, I adore, so it's not an indictment on them. It's just the scene as a whole, and the presence and posture of one of the guys specifically that shines a light on who the church is and where the church is going.)

The night before this couple would get baptized, a group of straight (mostly) white guys sitting around a table discussing the validity and sanctity of the baptism of these girls. Arguing over whether or not their baptism is valid, what God thinks about it, and what stipulations and conditions we should place on them, as pastors, if we are going to baptize them.

Stipulations.

Validity.

Conditions.

(Insert another Jesus facepalm here.)

Isn't it painfully hilarious how we are still having the same conversations about who is in and who is out, and who is clean and unclean thousands of years after Jesus dismantled and dismissed these so called boundaries.

Honestly.

It's so lame, and such a waste of our sacred energy.

And while so many people spend so much energy talking about these kinds of things, on that beach that beautiful afternoon, we were just doing it.

While other people were siting around trying to maintain the boundaries of insiders and outsiders, we were completely uninvolved in that conversation, fully engaged in life, and moving forward with the Spirit.

Same Spirit.

Same water.

Same bible.

Same prayers.

Same readings.

Same hopes.

Same dreams.

Same faith.

The stories of Jesus and these girls need to remind us that the Church is called to be the welcoming committee, not the managers of the guest list.

And if we can let go our conditions for acceptance, surrender our need to control other people's journeys, and liberate the Spirit to welcome as She sees fit, we will not only make room for so many other people at the party, we will experience so much more of the goodness of being included ourselves.

Ten

CREATIVITY/MAKING

It has been said that 90% of people live 90% of their lives on cruise control. What this means is too many people around us are sleep walking their way through life. Choosing the path of least resistance, silencing the voice within them that is crying out to become more, and gradually deciding that courage and creativity are not going to be a central part of their lives.

But for creatives, for artists, for entrepreneurs, for people who take their work seriously, for people who care about their craft and live intentionally, people who live from the depths of their heart and soul for their friends and family.

Which means people like you.

You have chosen a different path.

You have chosen to live a creative life, and you love it.

You capture, you film, you write, you sew, you design, you host, you take care of your family—you are a person that makes things and makes things happen. It's like you have this relentless need to take the raw materials of creation and to make something beautiful and meaningful out of it.

You know that creating is somehow connected to the deepest part of what it means to be human.

Our world is not a product, it's a project. It is not finalized and it is not static. It is dynamic, it is moving, and you are the ones that are intentionally committed to helping it become more of who she was created to be. Your projects are a part of the much larger process of the Spirit that is unfolding in, around, and through us.

You know this.

You are awake creatively, you know the joy of making things that matter. You understand that terrifying and liberating feeling of throwing yourself into something you believe in when you have no idea how it is going to turn out.

You know how good this life really is.

But—and this is a big but. Matter of fact, this is a seven foot four, four hundred pound Andre the Giant, black speedos circa 1986 sized but—you also know about how hard it is to keep putting yourself out there. You know what its like to feel stuck, to feel like other people are passing you by. To question whether you have what it takes to really make this work.

You know what it's like to feel alone in the creative process.

You also know about struggle, about pain, about the hard parts of the creative life that others don't understand. You know about feeling exposed, what it feels like to risk again and again and again, and sometimes you wonder whether any of it even matters.

There's a story about this young CEO of an innovative non-profit. This woman was highly driven and had that rare blend of bigger picture vision, acute attention to detail and direct implementation of imagination. She was compassionate to the people she served, good to her employees and co-laborers, a rising star in the non-profit sector, and she came home on a Thursday night and once again, she was just done.

Have you ever felt that before?

Just.

Done.

As she kicked off her shoes and opened a bottle of wine, she went full monologue for the next twenty minutes. During this unfiltered rant, thanks to the wine, the exhaustion, and the presence of her closest friend, she said so many things that not only connect with anyone that commits to create and build, but also gives us insight into how letting go and courageous creativity are connected.

"No one appreciates what I'm doing."

"Sometimes it feels like it seriously doesn't even matter."

"When people say they're going to show up and they don't, it frustrates me."

"So disappointing seeing people get excited, but never get committed."

"No one cares" ("I think you already said that.") "I'm saying it again!"

"It's so hard to keep giving your all to something as essential that other people treat as optional"

"I'm just tired of feeling alone and carrying this."

"I just don't know if I can keep doing this."

And her friend, with all of her experience with similar work, connection with this young CEO, and a deep understanding of how the journey goes responded by saying,

"Yeah. I know. Trust me. I know."

And after a long pause says,

"So you ready to plan out the next 6 months?"

To which this young CEO responds by saying, "Yes."

Sound familiar?

When we are taking risks and giving ourselves creatively to this world, sometimes we are going to slow down long enough to be able to hear this distant voice within asking questions like, "How long can I keep this up? How do I keep going? What am I doing?"

While we are working, we are going to wrestle with how to keep working without losing our joy, our inspiration, and even ourselves.

This is where letting go and the creative process need to become close friends. Because if we surrender what we need to surrender and let go of what we need to let go of along the way, these questions about how to keep going start to answer themselves.

If letting go is the key toward continuing to create, what do we need to let go of to have the courage and strength to keep going?

First, we have to let go of our attachment to outcomes, and embrace our life as an offering.

During this past season of my life, my simple prayer and mantra each morning as I wake up is this,

"May everything I consciously receive as a gift be poured out as an offering."

The vocational life, or how we use our voice in this world becomes simple when we can think about it in terms of gift and offering. Everything that is, everything we are, and everything we receive is a gift. And flowing out of that acknowledgment and experience, everything we create, and all the energy we use is an offering for the world.

No calculating how much people or life owe us.

No fear of how our offering is going to be perceived by others.

No comparison of our unique offering to the offering of others.

There is the receiving of a gift, which is life. And there is an offering of a gift, which is our life.

Terri Guillemets said, "Art is when you hear a knocking from your soul—and you answer."

The art of embracing a life of gift and offering is us answering that knock on the door of our life, and choosing to give everything we have for this world, and then simply letting it be.

But we all know it doesn't always feel that simple.

We struggle to believe that our unique offering matters or has something valuable to bring to this world. We are so in tune with this deep desire to give ourselves away for the sake of others, but there always seems to be something getting in the way of us doing this. We pour ourselves out over and over until it feels like we have nothing remaining, and we are left feeling exhausted, under appreciated, and holding on to that bitter cup of resentment.

We know we are giving everything we have, and when we look to what others are giving, or how they are creating, or where they are working, or who they are working with, we cannot help but feel like our offering is diminished or devalued.

Despite the simplicity of that sacred flow of gift and offering that Christ invites us into, the freedom to enter into and remain in that flow is a life long task for each of us.

The stand up comedian Patton Oswald talks about how the one thing he wishes for every stand up comedian early in their career is that they would bomb!

Think about that.

The one thing he wants for aspiring comedians is the last thing they want.

Why is that? Why would this prolific comedian want others to experience the worst case scenario in their craft?

It is because he knows that the more intensely and frequently this happens, the quicker the things they fear the most will come true. They will fail miserably, be utterly embarrassed and completely humiliated. And after this happens, they will be able to wake up, realize they're still alive, and that they can keep going.

The fear of failure will get in the way of embracing our life as an offering.

Patton Oswald understands this.

The late Carmelite nun, Bernadette Roberts brilliantly said that, "Crucifixion wasn't the hard thing for Jesus, the hardest thing was incarnation." The hardest thing is not being humiliated or crucified, it is giving yourself fully and freely knowing that you might be humiliated or crucified. You have no control while you're dying. But you do have control over whether or not you're going to be living before the dying.

Roberts knows that the courageous decision to truly live is going to determine the degree of truth in our offering.

Steven Pressfield, in his powerful book, *The War of Art,* says that we all have two lives "the life we live and the unlived life within us."

The life we live.

And.

The unlived life within us.

The life we live is our day-to-day existence. Our work, our relationships, our errands, our recreation, and the everyday grooves we find ourselves in. But while all of this is happening, there is also this unlived life within that consists of all of our dreams, conversations, ideas, businesses, relationships, adventures, and risks we've never lived out.

Creativity and letting go is about the refusal to accept the unlived life as a part of us.

Our ego's attachment to outcomes as a source of value is always going to be one of the greatest inhibitors to embracing our life as an offering, and a great barrier to the freedom and joy to keep going.

The second thing we need to let go of to be able to create and give our lives as an offering is comparison.

I know.

Not a novel idea.

Not revolutionary.

I'm with you.

But it is still one of the most powerful forces that fights against our courage and calling to create. And while overcoming comparison is by no means novel as an idea, it is absolutely revolutionary when it is lived.

Comparison is something most people can recognize, but very few can resist.

In 2016, I was sitting outside of a Stumptown Coffee with my wife and some of our closest friends talking and people watching.

No, I was not watching the weirdness of Portland, I was watching the busyness of New York City.

We were right around the corner from NYU, and were sitting down outside of Stumptown, and right on the edge of all of the kinetic energy.

Students rushing to get to class.

Fashionistas walking to the next boutique.

Doctors heading back to the hospital.

Tourists amazed to be in the city.

And everyone else headed to unknown destinations, and doing so quickly.

Sitting on some nearby steps, surrounded by all of this motion and bustling energy, was a young black woman one hundred percent focused on what she was reading. She was immovable and unflinching. It was almost jarring to see that degree of stillness right in the middle of that much motion.

As this was happening, all I could think was,

everybody is passing her by.

They are moving faster, they are accomplishing more, they are covering more ground, they are being more productive, and they are not only passing her by, but also getting ahead.

But at the same time, I also thought,

they are not going where she's going.

Why would it matter if people are moving faster than her if they're not going where she's going?

What difference does it make if someone passes her by when they're not going where she's going? How could someone else's accomplishments take away anything from her when they're not headed where she's headed? What would it matter if someone covers more ground than her when they're not doing what she's doing, saying what she's saying, or creating what she's creating?

This young woman was unshakable in her focus because nobody else around her was going where she was going.

So, every time we feel the impulse of our ego to compare ourselves with anyone, we have to remember, they are not going where we're going.

We remind ourselves they are not doing what I'm doing.

We re-focus our energy because they are not saying what we're saying.

In John 21:15-22, there is this powerful conversation between Jesus and Peter.

At the onset of this story, Peter was living in that heavy and haunting space you dwell in right after you completely blow it.

Peter, who was the most excited disciple in the bunch, had abandoned Jesus, and made a huge mistake. He denied his friend, and had left the movement and returned to what he was doing before.

It's easy to go backwards after we make mistakes.

And after Jesus returns to him, re-initiates their relationship, and graciously calls him back to his unique path, this is what happens:

Peter turned and saw that the disciple whom Jesus loved was following them. (This was the one who had leaned back against Jesus at the supper and had said, "Lord, who is going to betray you?") When Peter saw him, he asked, "Lord, what about him?"

Jesus returns to him after he betrayed him, and still calls him forward and says, this is your path. This is what it looks like for you to give yourself fully. This is what the music of your life sounds like when you live with your true voice. And Peter immediately looks at John, and says, "Well what about him?"

What about him?

Him?

What about him?

The creative life force of the universe was flowing directly through Jesus to Peter, forgiving him, reminding him of who he was, and calling him into his distinct path, and the first thing he does is focus on what someone else's path looks like.

Why did he do that?

Or here's an even better question:

Why do we do that?

Why is it when God asks us to be here, our minds are over there? Why when God invites us to do this thing, we're obsessed with those people over there doing that thing?

We think people are having more fun. We think people are happier. We think people are passing us by. We assume what they're doing matters more, and all of this is simply getting in the way of the joy that only comes from focusing on walking our own path and doing our own journey.

All of the energy we spend focusing on what they're doing takes away the joy that only comes from focusing on what we're doing.

Every impulse we have to compare ourselves with others is also an invitation to connect deeper with the God who offers the gift of our true self—which is the only vehicle that carries our real offering. When we allow ourselves to be drawn in by that delightfully dark voice of comparison, we think it's about wanting what they have, but it's really about knowing who we are.

There is a path of constant comparison, crippling envy, and trying to compete with others for a sense of validation. But there is another path of joy, one where we can focus on the substance of who we are and the quality of the work we do. A path where we are discovering our own voice, recognizing our own gifts, and waking up to the life changing fact that nobody else can give the world what we can give.

This path is defined by us living beyond the constant call of comparison, and embracing our life as the simple and sacred offering that it is. Our only job is to do that.

Trying to keep up with others is not the key to your success. Secretly competing with other people is not what wisdom looks like. Comparison is not going to set you free. Trying to prove yourself is not going to help you enjoy the work you are doing.

All of this can get in the way of embracing your life as the sacred offering it is.

This is why Merton said, "For me, to be a saint, simply means to be myself."

The addition of others does not subtract from who we are or what we give. We can let go of the need to compare because no one else's contribution can add to or take away from the unique offering of our own life for this world.

Or, we can trust Merton's words, and that the most sacred thing we can ever do is be and give ourselves.

Our lives are streams flowing in an infinite river of creativity, grace, and love.

And you can't subtract from infinity.

A sunset is the universal language of beauty. It has the power to startle us in a sacred way and make us stop everything we are doing. Somehow, it can sneak past all of our defense mechanisms and emotional armor and touch the human heart in a powerful way.

The vast horizon of colors, dynamic textures, and the seamless way the details merge together to create a unified visual experience.

We pause.

We sit.

We quiet our souls.

We listen.

We are in awe.

We smile.

We cry.

THE JOY OF LETTING GO

We never once regret taking the time to sit with a sunset.

And despite the captivating nature of the sunset, and depth of experience we have in her presence, most of the time, we ignore her. We don't always drink in her beauty, allow her to settle us in the way only she can, or even pay attention.

Sometimes the most grounding form of beauty presents herself to us, and we go back to scrolling on our phone. And as tragic as that might seem, here's the thing,

It doesn't matter.

The thing that is so inspiring about a sunset is that a sunset just gives itself fully and freely to the world. The sunset doesn't hold back because there's not enough people watching. The sunset doesn't refuse to show up because it feels under appreciated. She doesn't withhold dimensions of her beauty out of fear that the right people won't understand.

Never.

The sunset just offers everything she has to the world regardless of how other people respond to it. The beauty the sunset creates is not contingent upon how many people take the time to agree on its beauty. The sunset just keeps showing up and relentlessly, or even recklessly keeps giving everything she has to the world.

The great mystic and poet Hafiz said,

"Even

After

All this time

The Sun never says to the Earth,

KEVIN SWEENEY

"You owe me."

Look

What happens

With a love like that,

It lights the whole sky."

The same thing Hafiz claims about the unconditional giving of the sun is also true for the relentless beauty of the sunset.

The sunsets show us that this is exactly what it is like to creatively give our lives as an offering to the world. To relentlessly and recklessly give everything you have to this world, and to let go of anything that is getting in the way of our truth.

So may you let go of your attachment to the outcomes, surrender the need to go on those unhelpful trails of comparison, and may you give everything you have as freely as the sunset gives herself every night here in Hawaii.

Eleven

INNER AUTHORITY

I'm going to tell you a story about a thirty-five year old man in Portland crying in his car in a crowded parking lot.

But first, why is it that our cars are the site for some of our most epic cries? Whether we're slowly driving down the street, looking at our self in the rear view mirror while we're parked, or swinging at the dash board in a rage, the car seems to have this magical power to draw out our tears.

Perhaps the God who always hears the cry listens closely to the car.

Now back to this man.

Overwhelmed by the corporate culture of speed, stressed out from the constant expectations to produce, and having a moment where all of life seemed to be hitting him at once, this successful man gets up and leaves his office. He goes outside and beelines to his car, gets in, closes the door behind him, and let's loose with one of those classic car cries.

And this particular cry had an added dimension of intensity to it, because it involved another classic element to the car cry,

a loud verbal altercation with God.

During this divine and verbal wrestling match, one phrase came out of this man's mouth over and over at one point.

"God, you gotta get me out of here."

"You gotta get me outta here."

"You gotta get me outta here."

Which, is a deeply fascinating statement because it is loaded with so many assumptions about how God, life, and reality work.

Apparently, in this man's version of the world, God is the one who does things for him. God makes decisions upon his behalf, and ultimately has the power to determine how he is going to respond during life's toughest times.

He is not the one who makes decisions and has the power to re-shape his reality.

God is.

There in that car, you have a highly educated, intellectually sophisticated, and successful man who in some way, still feels disempowered. He still feels like he's a victim of his circumstances and that he is a passive recipient of the choices of the divine decision maker for his life. It even seems like he didn't believe or realize how much power he had to choose what happened next.

When he says, "God, you gotta get me outta here," I imagine the divine voice saying, "Go for it. You have the power to make a decision to do that right now. You can leave if you want."

We act like life's just happening to us, but we've been created to happen to life.

Let me share with you a deep suspicion I have had for a long time about many people's path with God. Much of what is communicated as religious obedience or spiritual piety is actually just passivity and disempowerment.

God has created us for creativity, but we prefer conformity.

God has created us for innovation, we prefer to gather more information.

God has created us for spiritual experience, we prefer living up to people's expectations.

When adults speak of obedience to God, so often, it sounds like children who are begrudgingly doing what is "right," even though beneath the surface, they would rather be doing something else. When I am in the presence of that language, it doesn't feel like the kind of freedom we have available to us in Christ.

So much of the language and culture of obedience comes from childish, immature, and passive ways of seeing ourselves and God

We long for the freedom to do what we want, but when those defining times come and we look ahead to the unknown, we still want someone to tell us what to do. We keep justifying where we are by telling ourselves that God has us exactly where he wants us, when the truth is that there were a thousand micro decisions we made along the way that steered us right to our current location.

We say we're waiting for God to speak, while God is waiting for us to choose.

Speaking of choices, let's take a look at the life of Moses briefly. Moses is the great liberator in the biblical narrative. Challenging the Egyptian Empire, speaking bone chilling truth to Pharaoh, and leading this mass political and economic liberation of the Israelites. He is the one responsible for revealing to the world that God is always in solidarity with the oppressed, and that any form of liberation that does not take injustice into consideration is nothing.

He is also the one who revealed that God always hears the cry, which is great for us every time we are breaking down in our cars.

Moses is a singular figure in the social and sacred history of the planet.

And when the writer of the book of Hebrews remembers Moses' greatness, they say this,

"By faith Moses, when he had grown up, refused to be known as the son of Pharaoh's daughter. **He chose** *to be mistreated along with the people of God rather than to enjoy the fleeting pleasures of sin."*

Moses chose.

That's it.

That is what made him great.

A choice.

Moses chose to be in solidarity with the oppressed instead of enjoying the endless pleasures provided at the table that was built on the backs of the oppressed.

So the historical greatness of Moses is defined by the simple reality of choice.

Moses is one of the most iconic, influential, and important figures in human history. A person whose name is synonymous with liberation, a person whose legacy has catalyzed more work for transformation in our world than almost any other human being, and the writer of Hebrews says he became that person because he chose to.

It wasn't magic, it was a choice.

It wasn't some uncontrollable fate, it was something he decided to do.

It wasn't a fixed plan that he just happened to fall into, it was a decision he made with his real everyday life.

Moses reveals the simple, but forgotten truth that we always have the power to choose.

(Even as I write this chapter right now, I'm looking at my computer screen, amused by the obvious idea that I could continue this part of the chapter in countless ways. This work, like everything else, is not the product of fate, it is the simply the expression of different choices I have made that have led me here.)

As people of the Spirit, we live with a daring sense of permission. We all carry a frightening and liberating sense of freedom to choose. Faith is an exciting invitation not to follow the rules, but to allow love and creativity to help us see beyond the need for rules into the holy horizon of possibilities.

There is a natural movement forward from passivity to power.

The further spiritual path ahead requires us to go from always seeing the governing authority in our life as being outside ourselves in religious leaders, parents, or the country, to recognizing the inner authority we have from the authorizing power of Spirit within.

When this starts to happen, life no longer feels like a divine tight rope or morality test, but a cosmic dance we enter into where we have the freedom to twirl to however the sound of the Spirit moves us. We are called forward to move from obedience to a commanding God, to innovation and creativity with a Present Spirit.

This expansive future is about us learning the sound of our own voice, tuning into the frequency of our unique desires, and learning to read the text that the Spirit is writing in and through our own life.

I know.

It's scary.

It's scary to know how free we actually are.

But it's also exciting, and liberating to realize how powerful we are.

So what does it take to live with this sense of inner authority? What gets in the way of this sacred freedom to choose? Why can it be hard to embrace this infinitely interesting way of being?

Or perhaps the better question is, what do we need to let go of to embrace our inner authority?

The first thing we need to let go of in order to live from this deeper place of inner authority is the need for reassurance or permission from external authority.

At eighteen, when I walked away from college sports and music, I failed to meet any expectation that every person in my life had on me. I disappointed so many people, received quite a bit of judgment and criticism as a result.

I moved to Hawaii to start over. Almost nobody understood or celebrated my decision, it seemed like I was making the biggest mistake of my life, and I knew exactly what I was doing.

The divine light switch that was turned on in me after my initial awakening encounter with God enabled me to see with clarity. This clarity gave me the ability to carefully discern between what I wanted, and what others wanted for me. The clearness of this new way of seeing allowed me to easily distinguish between the desires inside that were indigenous to the soil of my own spirit, and the ones that had been planted there by others. Which means I could spot the different feeling between what I wanted and what others wanted me to want, or thought I was supposed to want.

Only authentic inner experience of God gives us inner authority in our life.

This inner authority from Spirit means we begin to see with our own eyes, feel with our own bodies, know with our own knowing, and ultimately live our own lives. No religious leader can think our thoughts for us. No parental figure can see for us. No mentor or guide can feel our feelings for us, or participate in the intimate relationship we have with our dreams and desires. No person we look to as an expert will ever have the capacity to choose for us.

What could any external authority give me that the authorizing presence of the Spirit has not already given me?

When my wife and I first started Imagine, one of the key ideas we communicated to our team was this: we ask our elders for guidance and wisdom, but we never ask for permission.

Permission to do what we know we are here to do?

No.

Permission to do it the way we feel called to do it?

No.

Permission to be ourselves?

No.

Guidance? Yes. Permission? No.

This monumental shift toward inner authority is about waking up to that sacred and startling truth that no one else is here to give you permission.

And realizing that's a good thing.

To see how this natural movement from experience to authority takes place in the Scriptures, let's take a look at one of the prototypes of a life empowered by inner authority, and one of the original mystics in the Christian tradition, the apostle Paul.

Paul's spontaneous awakening with Christ happened with this sudden burst of light.

As he neared Damascus on his journey, suddenly a light from heaven flashed around him. He fell to the ground and heard a voice say to him, "Saul, Saul, why do you persecute me?"

"Who are you, Lord?" Saul asked.

"I am Jesus, whom you are persecuting," he replied. "Now get up and go into the city, and you will be told what you must do."

The men traveling with Saul stood there speechless; they heard the sound but did not see anyone. Saul got up from the ground, but when he opened his eyes he could see nothing. So they led him by the hand into Damascus. For three days he was blind, and did not eat or drink anything.

So while Paul is traveling, he is suddenly overwhelmed and shocked by this flash of light, identifies this light with Jesus, goes blind temporarily, and somehow becomes the leader of an entire movement which has Christ at the center.

Interesting.

Years later, as he looks back and reflects on this moment and attempts to make meaning of it in his letter to the Galatians, his words help give even more shape to this progression from experience to authority. In Galatians 1, Paul writes,

"Am I now trying to win the approval of human beings, or of God? Or am I trying to please people? If I were still trying to please people, I would not be a servant of Christ." (v.10)

"I want you to know, brothers and sisters, that the gospel I preached is not of human origin. I did not receive it from any man, nor was I taught it; rather, I received it by revelation from Jesus Christ." (v.11)

But when God, who set me apart from my mother's womb and called me by his grace, was pleased to reveal his Son in me so that I might preach him among the Gentiles, my immediate response was not to consult any human being. (v.15-16)

First, what happened?

Saul, the most oppositional force to this blossoming Jesus movement has this unprompted experience of and awakening with Christ.

Second, how does he describe his experience and his response to it?

He claims that the message of Jesus is not something he learned from any person or form of authority, but rather a direct receiving of and revealing from Christ.

He then goes on to audaciously say that he did not first respond by consulting any human being, that he is not looking for any approval from people or trying to please them, and he knows that God has called him by grace.

Authentic experience of Spirit.

No need for validation from authority.

No desire for approval from people.

Immovable confidence in the truth of what happened.

Paul's experience clearly shows us that the radical embrace of inner authority is only born out of the womb of inner experience. And that the confidence to stand up and move forward on the grounding nature of grace demands that we let go of the need for any form of external authority to validate our experience.

Letting go of the need for confirmation from the outside frees us up to trust the Christ of the inside.

(Of course I understand how this individualistic idea that it's just God and me can lend itself to some kind of self-assured, delusional, and abusive form of religious power where a toxic leader dangerously equates everything he does with divine permission.

But that's not what I'm talking about at all. And those guys are pretty easy to spot.)

In another letter to the Corinthians, Paul wrote, *"When I was a child, I talked like a child, I thought like a child, I reasoned like a child. When I became a man, I put the ways of childhood behind me."*

When you first begin to make that transition from placing ultimate trust in external authority and leaders, to trusting the inner authority and God's leading, there is a real sense of loss that arises. The stabilizing comfort that you used to receive from the affirmation or permission of authority figures like your parents, pastors, or anyone you allowed to sit on that seat of power in your life is taken away from you.

It's no longer as simple as,

"My dad says…"

"My pastor says…"

Or even "The Bible says…"

(Now, even God is no longer an object outside of me I look to for permission, God is a presence woven into me that I seek to be in creative and loving alignment with.)

But the good news is that the false sense of comfort you experienced from the certainty of trusting in authority is replaced with this deeper sense of excitement that comes from living into possibilities.

The more you let go of that childish need for affirmation from authority, the more you gain the sacredness and power of your own voice.

The second thing that needs to be surrendered and let go of to take ownership of our inner authority is the need for approval and acceptance from others.

One of the images I have used for a long time to describe this inescapable need for approval that is built into our human experience involves a river and dixie cups.

This divine dilemma is that each morning, every human being wakes up in the river, proceeds to get out of the river, and then spend the rest of their day begging others for dixie cups of water.

Of course in this image, the river is God, grace, Spirit, acceptance, unconditional affirmation, and absolute embrace.

(Feel free to add to or subtract from that list if it's helpful.)

So, each of us are born into the river, invited to trust the river, and are made whole through the healing waters of the river. And yet, our collective neurosis on our path to success, prioritization of perception over substance, and constant drive for positive feedback puts on display how little we trust and know our place in the river for ourselves.

This metaphor can become such a guiding vision for us as we seek to embrace our inner authority, because the need for approval and acceptance is one of the most daunting hindrances to trusting in our own voice.

Authenticity always requires us to let go of the need for approval.

Or, as Thomas Merton boldly wrote, "When ambition ends, happiness begins."

Now, it is clear through his own holy ambition and creative output, Merton did not mean that we are not to live with a great sense of purpose and drive (He wrote around fifty books!). We are here to build, we've been created to create, we are integral parts of the co-creating of this world and instruments of growth in the unfolding process of evolution.

Instead, the kind of ambition that Merton claims needs to end is the culturally shaped and toxic kind that is still being driven by the approval of others.

We can unapologetically create out of who we are without any need for others to get it.

We can share our lives with this world without giving a shit about the comments.

We can love this world and let the people who have problems with how we do it, just be.

This freedom emerges at the intersection of the divine affirmation of who we are, and the absolute acceptance of where others are.

We see the life of Jesus being one that is defined by him owning his own inner authority, and being met with a diversity of responses whenever he does.

In Mark 6:1-7, the gospel writer writes,

"Jesus left there and went to his hometown, accompanied by his disciples. When the Sabbath came, he began to teach in the synagogue, and many who heard him were amazed.

"Where did this man get these things?" they asked. "What's this wisdom that has been given him? What are these remarkable miracles he is performing? Isn't this the carpenter? Isn't this Mary's son and the brother of James, Joseph, Judas and Simon? Aren't his sisters here with us?" And they took offense at him.

Jesus said to them, "A prophet is not without honor except in his own town, among his relatives and in his own home." He could not do any miracles there, except lay his hands on a few sick people and heal them. He was amazed at their lack of faith

Then Jesus went around teaching from village to village."

Some were amazed.

Others were questioning him.

Many were offended.

A few even used his family heritage as leverage to discredit him.

Jesus goes into this place to be with these people, to share from the depths of who he is, knowing that not everybody is going to receive it, and that some are actually going to question and criticize him. And he still chooses to keep going and give himself freely to these people.

Do you know how hard that is?

How painful it is to really try, to really care, to really throw yourself into something and have people question you or criticize you? How excruciating it can be after you have your heart broken, to open back up again? After you've been betrayed, to choose to give yourself again? After you've seen things fall apart, to make that decision to keep moving forward?

But Jesus shows us, it's not about what other people say, its about you being true to what you see.

Right after this experience, Jesus begins to send his disciples out together. He sends them out to love how he loves, proclaim what he proclaims, and live how he lives.

He knows they're going to experience the same challenges, resistance, and bullshit as him.

And as he gathered his friends and disciples to prepare them for this journey, this is what he said:

"And if any place will not welcome you or listen to you, leave that place and shake the dust off your feet as a testimony against them." (Mark 6:11)

Jesus sends them out to do the same things he was doing, knowing they were going to face the same things he was facing. And when he sends them out to proclaim the Kingdom of God and to live out this new way, he says when people don't accept you, shake the dust off of your feet and move on.

He didn't say if they don't accept you, make sure you argue with them until they do. He didn't say if they don't like you or approve of your work, then do everything you can to try and win them over. He didn't say if they criticize you or don't get why you're doing what you're doing, then make sure when you go home you lose sleep obsessing over their lack of approval. He simply sent them out to live and share the truth.

People don't get it? That's dust.

They don't approve of how you're doing it? That's dust.

You fail to meet people's expectations? That's dust.

These experiences can feel so heavy, they can stick to us for a duration of time we are embarrassed to admit, and sometimes we allow them to have the power to silence our real voice, and deter our sacred work.

But if we do the divine work of real surrender of the need for approval, and let go of the need for acceptance, we will know for ourselves that all of the stuff that is getting in the way of our own voice, and blocking the power of our own authority, is in the end,

just dust.

Twelve

JOY

"I have told you this so that my joy may be in you and that your joy may be complete."

On the last night Jesus was going to spend with his disciples, and in what would become their final conversation, Jesus kept on talking about joy.

Not belief statements.

Not doctrine.

Not a list of rules.

But joy.

Not power.

Not war.

Not domination.

Deep joy.

Not success.

Not how to run a meeting.

Not unleashing productivity.

Jesus kept insisting that this entire mystery and all of this life is structured around joy.

It feels as if Jesus was saying, "The path I am showing you heads toward joy. The reason I have come is for joy. The place all of this leads when actually lived out is an experience that is defined by joy. The sacrifice, the love, the forgiveness, the honesty, the risks, the welcoming of others, everything I have showed you is about clearing the way for joy to emerge in your life and in our world."

This unexpected emphasis on joy seems to be central for Jesus, which then means it is at the center of life itself.

Joy?

Hmmm. Really?

Hard work? Okay. Meaning? Yeah. Success? Makes sense. Contributing? Of course.

But joy?

It's so simple that it's almost impossible.

My wife was having lunch with a friend who was going on about her exhausting schedule. From work, to school pick ups and drop offs, to extracurricular activities for her kids, to extended family responsibilities, to church stuff, to the constant queue of text messages that demand a response—she was tired, frustrated, and the state of being overwhelmed had become the normal resting place for her life.

After listening intently to the words and being present to the energy of her good friend.

THE JOY OF LETTING GO

To which her friend responded, "Joy? Who has time for joy?"

Sometimes we're too busy to even think about joy.

Have you ever heard of the justification mixtape? Well, even if you have never heard of it, I guarantee you have heard it playing.

The justification mixtape usually turns on in our head at night time when our creative output for the day is coming to an end, or when we are doing something fun during the day time. Whenever it comes on, it is our mind making a mental list of everything we accomplished, completed, produced, and did during the day for the sake of justification.

Which raises the essential question: What exactly are we justifying when we do this?

Our existence? Our right to live? Our ability to experience joy?

"Let's see. I worked for six hours. I responded to seven of those emails. I worked out for forty minutes. I filed most of that paperwork. I did some of my billing. I sent out all those orders…"

(You have your own version of this.)

And if the shape of the day meets our arbitrarily created criteria, we allow ourselves to rest a little bit and wind down for the day. If it does not, we hop back on our laptop, and do some version of work until we can stop producing and justify to ourselves (and it is always to ourselves) why we deserve to finally stop and enjoy.

In this way of being, joy and rest are earned based on output levels.

And let's be honest,

it's hard to experience joy when you feel the need to justify your existence.

KEVIN SWEENEY

In 2014, two Hamburg based photographers, André Giesemann and Daniel Schulz, created this photography series about the German club scene titled, "Vom Blieben," or, "What Remains." What was so unique and defining about this project was that the focus was not on the parties or the energy in the club while it was open, it was on the visual of the space when it was empty the morning after.

The artists said their goal for the project was to get, "people to reflect on their relationship with clubs." In an interview for the series, one of the photographers, when speaking of what it was like shooting the morning after some of the most sought after night club experiences in Germany, said, "...sometimes it's simply the emptiness that remains."

Which leads me to ask this question: Is he talking about the clubs or the lives of the people that were in them?

Sometimes we just keep partying, and assume that we must be filled with joy, without ever stopping to make room for the truth of our current state of being. Because we're having so much fun or experiencing so much pleasure during the experience, we can uncritically assume there is joy in the experience. But lasting joy has to be bigger than any particular experience.

We don't just want to feel like a different person for a night, we want to be a different person for our life.

We don't just want an intense experience, we want actual transformation that lasts.

We don't just want to be happy during the event, we want to have joy forever.

And people (like myself) who have spent their time at the university of drugs and reckless drinking, and eventually graduated all know something.

THE JOY OF LETTING GO

Partying is what you do when you hide from the pain, and joy is what happens when you find hope in the pain.

Let's stop right here.

Do you see how we already have a complicated relationship with joy?

We're too busy to even think about joy, we work hard in order to justify being able to rest and enjoy, and sometimes we keep can keep partying and make the mistake that joy in the driver's seat, when it's barely even along for the ride.

We want it, desire it, forget about it, or can't seem to hold onto it.

But, Jesus claims that all of life has been structured by love and built for joy.

Which brings us back to our constant companion of a question: What needs to be let go of in order to experience more joy?

The first thing we need to let go of in order to make more room for joy in our lives are attachments.

Attachments to what?

To everything.

Everything? That cannot possibly be what you mean.

Yes.

It is.

Everything.

Let's start with this idea of attachment itself.

Attachment is about clinging. It is needing something to be more than what it actually is, or needing it to give you more than what it is able to give. It is the ego's attempt to create value or establish security for itself outside of the ever present Spirit. Attachment is the experience of being over-identified with something, or some thing.

When it comes to attachment and joy, over-identification is an important term.

This is when we allow any sense of our value and identity to be attached to or contingent upon any thing external to who we are.

Attachment and over-identification are believing the lies of the ego that say

you are not truly you without that position,

you are not as valuable without being in this relationship,

you are nothing without getting all of that attention,

you do not matter without that job.

Calling us back to the past in order to move forward, Mirabai Starr brilliantly reminds us that "The mystics of all traditions and both sexes sing of the joy of burning. What burns? Our attachment to the false self."

When we let go of our attachment to the false self, we begin to have the freedom to dis-identify with any attachments of the false self.

At the beginning of the seventh year of Imagine, our church was in the healthiest place it had ever been. We had just transitioned into a great new space for Sundays, the co-creating dynamic was higher than ever, and there was this palpable momentum and energy in the community. And right as all of that was happening, I was sensing the possibility that our future might be somewhere other than Hawaii.

Everything was great. But I felt I was in a space where I had to put everything on the table, be willing to let go of any particular part of my life, and be open to the possibility of starting over.

And during my time in silence during this weird season, I just kept saying, "I can walk away from this. I am not Imagine. Imagine is what I give the best of my love and creative energy to, but it is not me. Imagine is the vehicle through which I am living out this life of love, but it's not who I am."

Now, before this is dismissed as not that big of a deal.

Keep in mind.

This is the church my wife and I co-founded when we were twenty-eight years old. A community we had given close to a decade to, sacrificed and risked for, and shed many tears over. This was the most central part of our vocational life.

It is so easy for our egos to be completely over-identified with our work. Especially if it is something you created and founded.

But still, letting go of any form of over-identification with Imagine through the years, and not being attached to Imagine for my sense of Self allowed me the freedom to envision a life beyond it, and trust if that was where the Spirit was leading me.

Now, when I went back to California that Christmas and drove around carrying the possibility of moving back, I realized I wanted to stay in Hawaii.

I love Hawaii and am not going anywhere.

But the important truth is that I had the freedom to leave the very thing I spent seven years of my life building, simply because I knew in the very cells of my being, that what I did was not who I am.

The You that is truly You is before and beyond any roles that you have.

You are not all of the things that are happening in your life, you are the steady current that is flowing through your life.

You are not anything that you can see, because you are only and always that which is seeing.

Who you are is eternal, always present, unmovable, and made of grace and love. You do not receive freedom from any particular form, because freedom is when you discover you are the space within which form itself arises. Every role your ego used to want to attach to for a sense of identity and value are now seen for what they are—temporary vehicles for love to flow into this world, instruments of the music of your life during this specific performance, and the wonderful waves you ride, knowing that this entire thing is about the joy of the ocean itself.

Letting go of our attachment to any thing is what frees us to be one with everything.

There's this powerful story about these two beautiful monks who lived in a monastery together, Abba Lot and Abba Joseph. One night, Abba Lot went to Abba Joseph and said to him, "Abba, as far as I can I say my little office, I fast a little, I pray and meditate, I live in peace, and as far as I can, I purify my thoughts. What else can I do?"

Then the old man stood up and stretched his hands toward heaven. His fingers became like ten lamps of fire and he said to him, "If you let go of your will, you can become all flame."

THE JOY OF LETTING GO

You can become all flame only by letting go of any form of attachment.

And I know.

It's hard.

It's scary.

It's painful.

It is a fresh experience of death and grief each and every time we surrender an attachment and let go of the part of us that we thought needed that particular thing.

That job.

That reputation.

That recognition.

That relationship.

Its always a form of death when we dis-identify with anything our ego was previously attached to.

Jesus dares to make the claim that "The kingdom of heaven is within you."

And in reference to this, Shane Hipps says so simply, "One kind of joy comes from the world outside, and another joy comes from a place inside."

The pure joy of the Kingdom of Heaven that always arises from within cannot be felt and known by us as long as we are attached to anything else.

The next thing we need to let go of in order to make room for more joy in our life is the need to avoid pain.

Let's go back to that conversation Jesus was having with his disciples that I began with. Like I already said, this instance in the gospel of John would end up being the last extended conversation Jesus was going to have with his friends and his disciples. And I mentioned that in this final conversation, Jesus centers all of the energy of life around joy.

What I didn't mention was the intensity of suffering Jesus was stepping into right after this conversation. This was the night before he was going to be crucified. The night before he was going to head to the cross that was held together by the personal pain of Jesus and the universal liberation of humanity.

While he was preparing himself for the promise of suffering, he was revealing to us the presence of joy.

In the middle of that heavy and holy space, this is what Jesus said to his disciples.

Very truly I tell you, you will weep and mourn while the world rejoices. You will grieve, but your grief will turn to joy. A woman giving birth to a child has pain because her time has come; but when her baby is born she forgets the anguish because of her joy that a child is born into the world. So with you: Now is your time of grief, but I will see you again and you will rejoice, and no one will take away your joy.

All of the mystery, all of the paradox, all of the distinct lines our mind want to draw between good and bad, pain and joy, and either or, are all collapsed into these words from Jesus, and into the Word of Christ.

Suffering builds the house of the sacred, loss is what gives us the clarity to see love, and pain clears out the path for joy.

This is why Father Rohr exclaims that the way of Jesus is, "...a story about believing someone can be wounded and resurrected at the same time!"

Wounded and resurrected.

Not wounded or resurrected.

Wounded *and* resurrected.

How many different ways do Jesus and all of the great mystics have to make this connection between grief and joy in order for us to accept it and commit to live it out as one of the central tasks of the entire sacred path?

Mirabai Starr says, "Mystics dwell in the zone between unbearable suffering and transcendent joy."

Gibran wrote, "Your joy is your sorrow unmasked. And the selfsame well from which your laughter rises was oftentimes filled with your tears."

Rumi said, "The wound is the place where the light enters you."

St. John of the Cross said, "...cry in prayer and the door will be opened in contemplation."

We spend so much of our life resisting some of the most natural relationships in life.

Pain and joy.

KEVIN SWEENEY

Suffering and love.

Hurt and hope.

Pain is not something we need to eliminate from our life, it is something we need to integrate in our life, so we can keep receiving the flow of joy through our life, as we learn how to embrace the presence of God as our life. We can let go of our need to avoid pain, because it is only when we do that we can see that

joy is the space where happiness and heaviness become one.

I live on the thirty-seventh floor of a building in the arts district neighborhood in Honolulu, called Kaka'ako. Our neighborhood is just on the edge of Downtown, three miles from the mountains, and two blocks from the beach. I cannot downplay the truth at all—the views here are amazing, and the sunsets we see on the regular will melt the heart of any novel eyes.

I love where I live.

It's my favorite place in the world.

One early evening around sunset, my wife and I were sitting together at a table on our lanai (that would be a balcony if you're reading this from the mainland) reading, listening to music, meditating, writing, or drinking wine as our way of maintaining a sense of sanity during Covid-19 with two small kids.

Sometimes we do all of these at the same time.

On this particular night, I glanced over at my wife and she had her AirPods in, a single tear streaming down her face, and her glass of wine close by. Now, was it the beauty of the horizon, the boundary breaking unity with the Spirit she felt, the loosening up from the wine, or the stress from the kids all day that lead to the tear?

Yes.

Yes it was.

But no matter what it was that was leading my lion of a wife to tears, as I turned back to the horizon and mountains, I could see pink rain pouring out of some clouds in the distance.

Pink.

Rain.

It was awesome.

As I sat with and let in the beauty of this unusual phenomenon, something deep within me said very calmly,

"This is only possible because of the light and the rain."

The light (which we normally see as good) and the rain (which we normally see as bad) formed a relationship that created a moment of beauty that transcended but included them both.

The beauty of pink rain formed through a relationship of two things the dualistic mind normally sees as good and bad. But the horizon was wide enough to hold it altogether and let it all be one thing.

We need to trust that the horizon of our own being is wide enough, and the love of God is deep enough to hold it all together within us too.

The life, death, and resurrection of Jesus form a seamless path that is wide enough to hold all of life together as one dynamic flow in the Spirit. As long as we don't deny, avoid, or reject any of it, we have the freedom and the power to embrace the paradox of death and life, and pain and joy.

Let the pain in, it's only visiting temporarily.

Sit with all the suffering, it can never outlast the presence of love.

Face all the heaviness of life, this where you come face to face with the holiness of God.

So, if you ever find yourself wondering,

Why does he talk about death so much? Because of how much I believe in life.

Why does he talk about pain so much? Because of how real joy is.

Why does he talk about the dark so much? Because of how much I trust in the light.

Why does he talk about the ending so much? Because of the perpetual possibility of beginning.

Joy is what emerges when you hold hands with darkness and light, and welcome them both in equally to be a part of your ongoing path.

Thirteen

FORGIVENESS

"Ever since I can remember, I've always had this anger just beneath what feels like the surface of my throat."

This handsome, funny, and articulate young man who was rapidly approaching thirty shared with his new therapist. As he continued to share about the rage that has driven some of his worst decisions, she began to see the sheepish and unsure inner world right behind his self-assured eyes. He would do anything for the sake of approval from peers or to belong. He could easily forget his own well being for the sake of making sure others were happy—which really meant to make sure they weren't mad at *him*.

He even shook the solid ground of this therapist with his tales of addiction, the time he spent living on the streets, the illegal schemes he had to provide for his habit, and what shame did to all of his relationships.

He named the countless issues that together created this toxic and twisted sense of life that felt impossible to begin to disentangle, even for a professional.

And after hearing everything this young man said, his new therapist responded and said,

"You need to forgive your mother."

Our relationship with forgiveness is a lot like our relationship with letting go. Which makes sense because forgiveness is impossible without letting go. The similarities I am drawing here are about how we can convince ourselves that the core of our struggle is about a million small things other than the simple step of forgiveness waiting to be taken.

Just like we do with letting go.

Whenever we feel stuck, we are not stuck, we probably just have something really hard we need to do. And often times, that hard thing we need to do is called forgiveness.

Approaching the path of forgiveness can make us shutter and feel paralyzed. Developing the clarity to see this path as the only way forward at specific junctures of our life can deplete even our most courageous resources. We aren't always convinced we would survive this passage through forgiveness.

But to not forgive is to deny the heart of the narrative that runs through the storyline of humanity.

It would be to creatively dance around the center of Jesus' journey.

And to disqualify ourselves from the joy and life that makes this world good.

Now, before we romanticize it, lets be honest. To forgive is to embrace one of the most brutal and glorious parts of being human.

Brutal because of the violent way your mind, heart, and body can react to it.

Glorious because of the radiance and freedom on the other side of it.

When Jesus spoke of forgiveness (which he did quite often), he used this interesting Greek word "Aphiemi." Aphiemi is this layered and multi-dimensional word that can mean,

to release,

to let something be,

to send away,

and to ultimately forgive.

Can you see the possibility of an entirely new way of being just from this one word? Can you feel the tension start to loosen if you trusted in every release? Do you sense the peace start to arise within if you allowed everyone and everything to just be, through the act of forgiveness? Can you imagine the joy that would remain if you could send away every uninvited visitor carrying discomfort that was trying to make their home in your heart and body?

Do you understand the power of forgiveness Jesus invites us into?

Dr. Ellen Weber writes that,

"Forgiveness literally alters the brain's wiring – away from distortions brought about by the past, and beyond fears that limit the future. It leads from misery of a broken promise, to wellness that builds new neuron pathways into physical, emotional and spiritual well being."

Jesus teaches how forgiveness reveals the design of the heart, Weber shows what it does to structure of the brain.

Forgiveness is spiritual and biological.

Forgiveness transforms our brains and our futures.

Forgiveness is conceived in the depths of our heart, flows through the grooves of our brains, and is born into the world as a liberated form of love and a steady stream of creativity.

One of the self imposed rules I have while preaching at our church Imagine, is that I only get to talk about the movie Good Will Hunting once a year.

Okay. Maybe twice a year.

The limitations on Good Will Hunting references are a result of my personal love for it, the ways it cracks open the exterior shell of so much of our lives, and the power it has to draw us into something more expansive. And since I mentioned it in the first book (almost immediately in the introduction), I will now publicly establish the boundary of only mentioning it once in each book I write.

Well. Maybe twice.

The main character Will was an anomaly of a genius who lived on the sidelines of life.

Watching.

Reading.

Analyzing.

Critiquing.

Observing.

All of the information he gathered, knowledge he gained, and expertise he acquired was an unconscious way to stay distant relationally and unavailable emotionally. No matter how much he dreamed of a bigger future, or how deeply he desired to enter into the arena of life, there were barriers within him that prevented him from this alternate future.

The story is him slowly moving from the edges of his own life, to the center of life itself.

The apex of the movie is a scene with Will having a life altering break through with his therapist, played by Robin Williams (If you've seen it, you already know where I'm going).

Nearing the end of a long journey together in therapy, in this defining moment, Will's therapist gently but firmly approaches him and keeps repeating the phrase,

"Its not your fault." Will half smiles an uncomfortable smile young men make while an interaction becomes too real and says, "I know."

"It's not your fault." Will smiles again and says the same thing with a bit more irritation.

"It's not your fault." As his therapist gets closer this time, Will pushes him away and tries to get him to stop.

And when the therapist says it one more time while leading with a loving embrace:

After all the trauma and the complications.

After all the anger and resistance.

After all the feeling of being stuck with no with way forward.

Will finally lets go and weeps with the force of the universal repressed and hidden emotions just beneath the surface of all young men in our world.

It wasn't enough for him to simply see the path ahead. It wasn't enough for him to understand the power of forgiveness. It wasn't enough for him to even believe in the potential he had within.

He could see and understand all of that because of his intellect.

He had to walk the path of forgiveness himself, he had to accept the truth of his own life, and he had to be willing to let go in order to feel the power of freedom that would lead him to a changed life. And this scene was the site of Will being born again. Which ultimately gave birth to him moving away, pursuing love, and getting off the sidelines of his life for the first time.

He didn't need more knowledge and understanding, he needed to let go and forgive.

When referring to the difference between understanding and unfolding, Mirabai Starr says, "While we may comprehend that holding onto resentments is like ingesting spiritual cyanide, it is not easy to let go of the story line of our own wounds."

While it is easy to believe in the necessity of forgiveness, it is not so easy to let go, accept, and actually forgive what needs to be forgiven for ourselves. We do not forgive people by learning and understanding with our minds, we forgive people by letting go and allowing this unfolding to happen from the ground of our heart and the fullness of our bodies.

Forgiveness is always the way forward.

And if this is true, what is it then that keeps getting in the way of the liberating power of forgiveness?

What makes it so damn hard to forgive?

What do we need to let go of in order to forgive?

One of the most important things we need to let go of in order to forgive are our illusions.

Complete transparency here.

This is also one of the most agonizing experiences.

Let me begin by mentioning something about icons in the ancient Christian tradition. Icons are not something you look at, they are something you look through. An individual icon is not just a piece of religious art, it is a sacred doorway to the presence and beauty of God.

Linette Martin, in her book, *Sacred Doorways: A Beginner's Guide To Icons*, claims, "An icon is a two-way door of communication that not only shows us a person or an event but makes it present." So, an icon is something you look through to not only see the presence of God, but actually becomes the place where the Presence of God becomes present.

In the same way icons can become a dynamic reality you look through as a sacred window into the presence and beauty of God, each individual opportunity of forgiveness can become an icon you see through in order to get a clearer vision of your illusions.

Stay with me.

Each individual experience of forgiveness can reveal a universal illusion you still have about life. The individual experience is something you can look through in order to see broader illusions you are still holding onto in your life. Which means, you can see what is getting in the way of your life.

Yes it's about the individual, but it's also about our illusions.

Each time we forgive, we can unmask the unique experience and expose the truth of the universal illusion.

The connection between individual forgiveness and illusions is also why we fight forgiveness so hard. Every time the need for forgiveness forcibly sits down next to us, it subtly whispers, "this doesn't all work the way you thought it was supposed to does it?"

If you get close enough to the face of forgiveness, you can see your illusions.

The potential end of a relationship is so hard because it challenges your illusion that if you give everything you have to someone, it's always going to work out. The relationship is the individual event, the belief that things are always supposed to work out if you give your best is the illusion.

Forgiving your father again for what he did is undermining your illusion that if a dad really loved his daughter, he could never be that selfish and hurt her like this. Forgiving your father this time is the individual occurrence, believing that a loving dad could never hurt his daughter is the illusion.

Accepting and forgiving the hurtful criticism you received for your creative output denies the illusion that you can publicly create something meaningful without dealing with negative feedback. The criticism is the individual happening you have to accept in the moment, realizing you can never create without dealing with criticism is the reality you have to accept in life.

I could use many other examples that would connect almost exactly with the illusions of your own life, but you get the point.

The particular exposes a pattern.

The unique draws us into the universal.

The individual helps us see the illusion.

Each time you forgive someone for what they did, it's an invitation to accept reality for what it is.

In the middle of a conversation with a friend, she tells me that someone who used to be a part of our church was trashing me and Imagine at a different friend's home. As I listened, a jolt of hot and uncomfortable energy shot through my body and eventually settled into my stomach.

Here's a question before I tell you the whole story: When you get offended or hurt, how does it initially hit you on a bodily level? Does it pulse through you entire body? Is it a warm and rising energy that feels like it's simmering right around your throat and neck? Do your arms tingle? Is it a pulling weight that brings you down, or a rising rage that makes you want to react?

Getting offended and hurt always registers in our body. Mine initially shows up as warm energy in my chest area and a slight tightening at the bottom of my throat.

Now back to my story. Someone I did my best to love, never had a falling out with, and whose presence I valued in our community is now criticizing and attacking me in front of others.

Okay.

When I heard this story and imagined the scene, this is where the initial hurt and offense I began explaining barged in. I imagined the scene my friend described—this person who I know saying negative things about me, the group of people there listening to what they were saying, the comments and conversations, the possibility of being misrepresented, and that entire scenario happening without me knowing exactly what was said, and with no way to defend myself.

You ever have something like that happen?

It's a horrible feeling.

Our ego contracts, our body reacts, and our mind starts coming up with countless ways to defend ourself. We want to explain to everyone there why that other person is wrong or bad. We want to tell our side of the story. We want to present our case. We want, no we need to do everything we can to make sure that we are not being misrepresented or misjudged to all those people.

See, what I had to forgive was this one person criticizing me.

But what I had to let go of was the illusion that you will always be able to control how other people perceive you.

And in order for me to let go of that illusion in a fresh way,

I had to accept that in some people's story, I might be the bad guy.

I had to accept that all of those people there might perceive me in a negative light.

I had to accept that sometimes I'm going to be misrepresented and unable to defend myself.

The individual criticism was hurtful, but the acceptance of these realities, and letting go of the illusion that you can always control how others perceive you was actually the hardest part. Forgiving the individual was a fresh invitation to let go of any illusions I had about needing to manage the perception of myself to others.

The individual hurt always stings, but the illusion is what keeps us stuck.

In order to forgive them, I had to die to and let go of that illusion. Wrestling with forgiveness isn't just about the inability to accept what is happening to us in any moment, it is the struggle to not turn away and deny a larger truth about life itself.

We always fight to hold on to our illusions, but each time we do, we discover we never needed them in the first place.

And one of the most powerful discoveries you can make in this process of waking up is every single time you let go of an illusion, you become more free, you become more you, because ultimately you become more of Christ.

This is why Johannes Tauler, the great mystic and disciple of Meister Eckhart dared to say, "The soul has a hidden abyss untouched by time and space."

Letting go of our illusions feels like we are falling into an abyss.

Because it is.

But what Tauler teaches us is that it is in this sacred abyss, we discover the immovable center of our own being, the ground of all existence, and the felt experience of the truth of being in Christ.

We all learn that you have to let the pain in so you can let the past go, but we also have to lay our illusions down in order to pick the future up.

The second thing we need to let go of in order to forgive is the need for power.

For some reason we need to be reminded that at the heart of the Christian tradition is a crucified savior. Not a violent and conquering warrior. Not a truth bending and manipulative politician. Not a ruthless and rapacious CEO. And not an attention seeking and shameless celebrity.

A crucified savior.

This cosmic turning point taking place in and through Jesus is an excess of wisdom, and provides a beautiful lens to view the truth about power, love, and forgiveness.

From that crucified and powerless position, Jesus draws from a deeper power and is able to say, "Father forgive them for they do not know what they are doing."

Something profoundly unorthodox and unfamiliar allowed Jesus to have compassion on the very people who were responsible for crucifying him. What did Jesus have to accept and embrace in order to see humanity with the ever-present eye of compassion, even while they were crushing him and trying to get rid of him?

The ultimate act of forgiveness came from the excruciating embrace of powerlessness.

But powerlessness sounds weak and vulnerable. Our minds react, our hearts coil up and close down, and our egos contract at the thought of embracing this irresponsible form of weakness. Perhaps this is why, when reflecting on the Apostle's creed, Rohr writes, "twice we are reminded that God is almighty, yet nowhere do we hear mention that God is also all suffering and all vulnerable."

If we are unable to accept powerlessness as a part of our own life, we could never embrace it as a part of the heart of God.

And yet, we have to make peace with the reality that forgiveness always involves letting go of power.

Forgiveness is so hard because it makes us feel so vulnerable. And to be even more honest, forgiveness is hard not simply because it makes us feel vulnerable, but because in it, we truly are vulnerable.

The powerlessness that is required for forgiveness is the act of laying down all of the weapons we normally carry around to prevent ourselves from being wounded.

This is the sacred act of being unguarded.

Daring to hold that space where we are undefended, open, and accessible is one of the essential tasks for the freedom we are seeking. This refusal to defend or clamp onto any form of power that protects us from the vulnerability of powerlessness is one of the last things we learn how to do, and one of the things we need the most.

THE JOY OF LETTING GO

But it is in this powerlessness, we first begin to touch real power.

While we are undefended, we discover the truth of how safe we are. Sitting in a position of vulnerability for an extended time is what draws divine strength into our being in a way nothing else can. Surrendering the fragile ego's need to defend and fight back in order to maintain control, is what allows the Spirit to defend you and fight for you. Which is actually the discovery that there is no need to fight at all.

This is why the apostle Paul says, "That is why for Christ's sake, I delight in weaknesses, in insults, in hardships, in persecutions, in difficulties. For when I am weak, then I am strong."

This is where we know for ourselves, what Mirabai Starr means when she writes, "Our vulnerability is our strength. Our capacity to forgive is our superpower."

This why Ghandi turned our perspective of forgiveness upside down when he said, "The weak can never forgive. Forgiveness is the attribute of the strong."

Seeing the cross as the site of divine clarity concerning forgiveness, power, and strength upends our way of seeing, and invites us to take this massive step of transcending our ego's need to fight, to protect, and maintain our own defensive notion of power.

Weakness (or what we used to think was weakness) is where all the wisdom is.

Vulnerability is the birth place of real strength.

And the safest place to be in the universe is when you surrender all your need for power and control.

Forgiveness always involves letting go of power, and the divine surprise is realizing that this is a good thing.

The master story teller Peter Rollins wrote this parable of a unsuspecting priest that puts on display the kind of love that is only possible after we overcome our need to defend ourselves and our need for power and control.

This story was about a priest served and gave his life to the streets in the shadow of an empire. And as he gained the respect of the people while he selflessly cared for those in need, he also obtained the resentment and hatred of the King's son. This jealous prince and his vendetta against the church and the priest had a history of harassing and imprisoning church leaders.

Rollins tells the rest of the story powerfully.

The prince harbored a burning desire to put a stop to the priests work, but he did not want to garner the hatred of the people. So he carefully devised a plan that he believed would expose the hypocrisy of the priest to everyone in the empire once and for all.

He is a poor man thought the prince I will offer him a great sum of money in exchange for a public confession concerning his hypocrisy and the hypocrisy of his church.

So late one evening under the cover of darkness, the prince visited the priest and upon entering his home said "I have the power to reach every person in this kingdom through the printed press. For 10,000 rupees, would you write a letter to be disbursed throughout the kingdom in telegrams and newspapers informing people that you were nothing but a liar and a hypocrite?"

The priest was indeed a poor man who had been born into poverty and had no nothing but need all his life he thought carefully for a few minutes before finally responding. "I will do as you ask but only under three conditions. "

"What are your conditions?" Reply the prince.

"First if I do this you must leave me and my church alone."

"Yes, "said the prince."

Second you must release those brothers and sisters of mine who are innocent of any crime."

"It will be done, "replied the prince. "And your Third stipulation?"

"Well, "said the priest after a great deal of thought, "10,000 rupees is a great deal of money, and I am but a poor man. You will have to give me time to raise it."

The Prince is leveraging his power in order to manipulate the priest and expose him as a hypocrite to the masses, which would ultimately destroy his reputation.

The Priest has no need for power, spends zero energy trying to maintain the facade that he is perfect and is without flaws, and saw this exposing as a form of self-disclosure he could freely choose for the benefit of those he deeply cares about. Even to the point where he was willing to raise the money that the prince offered to him in order to make it happen!

This holy man overcomes the power of the prince because he has first overcome the need for power within himself. The strength he has gained from embracing weakness, and the power he has discovered in his own powerlessness has liberated him to love this world in a way that is virtually impossible for most of humanity.

To forgive requires you to let go of your need for power in the moment, and each time you do this you are closer to overcoming your need for power as a whole.

Fourteen

OUTRO

I am finishing this book as I approach the edge of a long and beautiful chapter of my life. As I move into the tenth year of the church my wife and I co-founded, I can feel my mind, heart, and body preparing for the end.

This is a community we risked our lives for and gave our hearts to for a decade, and I know its time is coming.

This is a family that we have welcomed into our home. A church that began with a group of dreamers who were willing to take risks, push buttons, transcend boundaries, challenge the status quo, and trust that the terrain of this new future we were leading them into was good.

This is a story with so many unforgettable and unlikely people coming together to create a church that is so unique. It is impossible to capture with words what my heart feels or how my heart carries this community within.

The great Rumi said, "When you do things from your soul, you feel a river moving in you, a joy."

Imagine has been the source of so much of the energy of this river of joy flowing within me for almost ten years.

And now it's time to let go.

This is a big form of letting go.

This morning I am finishing up the last part of writing for this book. It is Christmas time in 2021, it is a rare cold day for us here in Hawaii (and by cold, I mean 75 degrees), and I drove up to this beautiful spot in the mountains to sit at my favorite table and have this quiet, ceremonial moment to finish the book.

And as soon as I sat down to write, a state worker turned on his leaf blower and walked right near my table and proceeded to destroy the very silence I came here for.

I immediately said out loud to myself, "C'mon bruh."

And after an initial trigger of frustration, I formed that subtle smile that has been organically passed down through the perennial tradition, laughed to myself, and then let go one more time as I finished this writing journey about letting go.

Once again, letting go of the way things are supposed to go became the open door to the sacred pattern of what is.

This is a small form of letting go.

Letting go is both.

It's big and small.

It's the massive thing you gave ten years of your life to, and the little, hidden desire you had to write in silence.

But no matter how massive things look, how heavy parts of life feel, or how impossible an intersection of your life seems, letting go is always the way.

Always.

THE JOY OF LETTING GO

Always.

Always.

To let go is always to be more unified with God.

What else do you want?

BOOKS REFERENCED

Douglas Carlton Abrams, Dalai Lama, Desmond Tutu, *The Book of Joy: Lasting Happiness in a Changing World* (New York, NY, Avery, 2016)

Adyashanti, *Resurrecting Jesus: Embodying the Spirit of a Revolutionary Mystic* (Boulder, CO, Sounds True, 2014)

Richard Beck, *Unclean: Meditations on Purity, Hospitality, and Mortality* (Eugene, OR: Cascade Books, 2011)

Cynthia Bourgeault, *Wisdom Jesus: Transforming Heart and Mind—A New Perspective on Christ And His Message* (Boston, MA: Shambhala, 2008)

Cynthia Bourgeault, *The Heart of Centering Prayer: Nondual Christianity in Theory and Practice* (Boston, MA: Shambhala, 2016)

Ilia Delio, *Making All Things New: Catholicity, Cosmology, Consciousness* (Maryknoll. NY: Orbis, 2015)

Matthew Fox, *Meditations with Meister Eckhart* (Rochester VT, Bear & Company, 1983)

Mohandas K. Ghandi, *All Men Are Brothers* (New York, NY: UNESCO and The Columbia University Press, 1958)

Kahlil Gibran, *The Prophet* (New York, NY, Alfed A. Knopf, 1923)

Madame Guyon, François Fénelon, Père La Combe, *Spiritual Progress: Instructions in the Divine Life of the Soul, A Collection of Five Essays by Three Great Religious Thinkers* (Paris, FR: Adansonia Press, 2018)

Hafiz, Could not locate origins of Hafiz quotes.

Thich Nhat Hanh, *Living Buddha, Living Christ* (New York, NY: Riverhead Books, 1995)

Thomas Keating, *The Human Condition: Contemplation and Transformation (New York, NY: Paulist Press, 1999)*

Carl McColman: *The Little Book of Christian Mysticism: Essential Wisdom of Saints, Seers, and Sages* (Minneapolis, MN: Broadleaf Books, 2021)

Thomas Merton, *New Seeds of Contemplation* (New York, NY: New Directions, 1961)

Thomas Merton, *No Man is an Island* (New York, NY: HarperOne, 2002

John Phillip Newell, *The Re-Birthing of God: Christianity's Struggle for New Beginnings* (Woodstock, VT: Christian Journeys, 2014)

Henri Nouwen, *Compassion: A Reflection on the Christian Life* (New York, NY: Image Books 1982)

Henri Nouwen, *The Way of The Heart: Desert Spirituality and Contemporary Ministry* (Seabury Press, 1981)

Steven Pressfield, *The War of Art: Break Through the Blocks and Win Your Inner Creative Battles* (New York, NY: Black Irish Entertainment, 2002)

Bernadette Roberts, *What Is Self?: A Study of the Spiritual Journey in Terms of Consciousness* (Boulder, CO: Sentient Publications, 2005)

Richard Rohr, *The Divine Dance: The Trinity and Your Transformation* (New Kensington, PA: Whitaker House, 2016)

Richard Rohr, *Falling Upward: Spirituality for the Two Halves of Life* (San Francisco, CA: Jossey Bass, 2011)

Richard Rohr, *The Universal Christ: How a Forgotten Reality Can Change Everything We See, Hope For, and Believe* (New York, NY, Convergent, 2019)

Rumi, If you can find the origins of Rumi's beautiful words, well done.

Huston Smith, *Tales of Wonder: Adventures Chasing the Divine, an Autobiography* (New York, NY: HarperOne, 2009)

Mirabai Starr, *God of Love: A Guide to the Heart of Judaism, Christianity and Islam* (Rhinebeck, NY: Monkfish, 2012)

Mirabai Starr, *Wild Mercy: Living the Fierce and Tender Wisdom of the Women Mystics* (Boulder, CO: Sounds True, 2019)

Gabriel Uhlain, *Meditations With Hildegard of Bingen* (Rochester, VT: Bear & Company, 1983)

Simone Weil, *Gravity and Grace* (New York, NY: Routledge Classics, 1947)

Ken Wilber, *Grace and Grit: Spirituality and Healing in the Life and Death of Treya Killam Wilber* (Boston, MA: Shambhala, 1991)

Ken Wilber, *The Eye of Spirit: An Integral Vision for a World Gone Slightly Mad* (Boston, MA: Shambhala, 2000)

Ken Wilber, *Integral Psychology: Consciousness, Spirit, Psychology, Therapy* (Boston, MA: Shambhala, 2000)

KEVIN SWEENEY

Ken Wilber, *One Taste: Daily Reflections on Integral Spirituality* (Boston, MA: Shambhala, 2000)

For more information about Kevin Sweeney,
or to contact her for speaking engagements,
please email kevin@imaginehi.org or @kevinsweeney1.

QUOIR

Many Voices. One Message.

Quoir is a boutique publisher
with a singular message: *Christ is all*.
Venture beyond your boundaries to discover Christ
in ways you never thought possible.

For more information, please visit
www.quoir.com

CPSIA information can be obtained
at www.ICGtesting.com
Printed in the USA
LVHW081556180123
737309LV00008B/899

9 781957 007366